The Trusted Financial Adviser

The Secrets to a Long and Successful Career as a Financial Adviser

Lee Clarke

The Trusted Financial Advisor

First published in 2009 by;

Ecademy Press

6, Woodland Rise, Penryn, Cornwall, UK. TR10 8QD

info@ecademy-press.com

www.ecademy-press.com

Printed and Bound by; Lightning Source in the UK and USA

Set in Warnock Pro and Arial Narrow by Charlotte Mouncey

Printed on acid-free paper from managed forests. This book is
printed on demand, so no copies will be remaindered or pulped.

ISBN 978-1-905823-53-6

Acknowledgements

A fundamental concept may be the product of a single mind; a good book is rarely so. I would like to thank the following people who have helped me in so many ways to bring this book into being. Dan Sullivan, creator of the Strategic Coach® Program, Andi Lothian of Insights Training & Development, Kathy Kolbe of Kolbe Enterprises Inc, Tony Gordon, Jeremy Hoyland, John Shorter, Danby Bloch, my book coach Mindy Gibbins-Klein, Laura Morris for typing the original draft book, Charlotte Mouncey for designing and laying out the book and so patiently dealing with my various corrections, Dylan Sutton for his excellent illustrations and my son Simon and daughter Amanda who inspired me to write the book and last but not least to my wife Morwenna for so patiently putting up with the many weeks I've been writing.

Contents

Preface

As the world emerges from one of the most serious economic crises since the Wall Street Crash of 1929, the importance to people of having of a trusted, knowledgeable and professional financial adviser is greater than ever. The fact is, wherever you go in the world today it is clear that the financial security and well- being of communities, wherever they are on the globe, will depend on individual financial security. In Europe, where national social security systems have previously provided for the sick and the retired, the system is acknowledged to be broken. Further afield in Asia and the Far East where, in the past, families have tended to look after one another, the social model is changing and people no longer want or expect to be financially dependant in old age on their own children.

In the UK, the 1970s and 1980s saw the growth of an extremely successful financial services industry with a corresponding increase in the amount of individual personal savings. Concern about lack of professionalism among a minority of individual practitioners, coupled with dubious sales training in some of the larger banks and insurance companies, led to the birth of the most cumbersome regulatory regime anywhere in the world. Whilst this did have the effect of ridding the financial services sector of the worst offenders, the nature of the regime led to bureaucracy at a level which resulted in the virtual elimination of the direct sales distribution channel, and a massive increase in the cost of delivering financial advice and the associated products. It is no coincidence that as the numbers of people giving advice fell to an all-time low, there was also a dramatic fall-off in the amount of individual savings, retirement provision and the purchase of life insurance and income protection.

When Western-style democracy arrived in the former Eastern Europe so did the banks and life insurance companies who were keen to set up sales forces to exploit the new-found financial freedom in these developing areas. As I travelled around the world speaking at various conferences in these countries I was saddened to see history repeating itself, some of the same problems beginning to emerge that we had seen in the UK in the mid 1980s. Travelling further afield to Asia and India in particular it was clear how much of an impact a well-trained, highly professional financial adviser is already achieving, just one client at a time, in helping to bring prosperity and financial security to these emerging economies.

Speaking to these audiences, I impressed upon the enthusiastic men and women I met in financial services around the developing world that by growing their practices in an ethical way, always placing the interest of their clients above their own, they would become regarded in the same way as the very best doctors and surgeons within the community. They would also help prevent the decimation of their own profession that could arise, just as it did in the UK, through over-regulation if bad practices were allowed to continue unchecked.

Now that the UK has a robust regime in place to ensure fair play, the emphasis has turned to professional qualifications. Laudable though this is (and I do support the initiative), the many thousands of qualified lawyers, architects, accountants and even doctors who have been prosecuted in a criminal court for abusing or exploiting their clients proves that qualifications offer no indication as to integrity and that there is a higher and far more valuable requirement that our clients seek when looking for advice across all professions: that of being trustworthy.

On top of this, the requirement for academic ability over and above sales ability has brought about another change. In the past it was taken as read that anyone looking for a career in financial services would have a natural talent for building relationships and would therefore be able to build their own client bank. It was just that some were superb at it and some had to work harder to achieve success. Now the situation (in the UK at least) is quite the opposite. Talented, qualified advisers are often unable or even unwilling to prospect for and acquire new clients and, as a result, they spend their lives working for someone else at well below their actual potential because they simply do not know how to prospect. This is rarely taught any more; and for reasons that are beyond me, the word *selling* has been vilified in the UK. Yet, persuading a client to appoint you as a financial adviser is a sales process. Many insurance products are illogical on the face of it and are rarely bought without the intervention of a sales person. There's and old adage '*Life insurance is sold, not bought*'. This in no way denigrates life insurance, it's simply a reflection of the fact that family life cover protecting someone other than the person paying the premiums is less likely to be purchased without at least a recommendation from a professional intermediary.

In writing this book I have tried to keep the content generic and applicable as far as possible anywhere in the world.

I am indebted to many friends and fellow professionals who have been an inspiration to me and helped me to shape my business. I am also particularly appreciative of my clients who have allowed me to be part of their lives for so many years and who have enabled me to see the real value of the products and services they have chosen with my help and which have provided them with financial support at times of serious ill health, upon retirement and on the untimely death of a loved one.

The Demonisation of Selling

To be a good financial adviser offering advice to someone else's clients, technical competence is without doubt the single most important factor. To build your own financial services practice, however, requires far more. This book is aimed at people who want to work for themselves, building their own businesses rather than spending their lives working for someone else and building someone else's capital value and someone else's future. So let's tackle this head on: we have to be able to sell! The clients that younger IFAs in the UK typically advise are someone else's. Someone else sold those people on the merits of becoming a client. Whether it was a bank or a national IFA or perhaps a one-man band who sold his practice to another company, or benefited from a buy-out deal from his insurance company, someone obtained those clients using sales skills.

One of the saddest aspects of the current UK financial services model is that almost no training is available in the mainstream on how to build a business and how to find new clients - in fact in almost every skill necessary to build a business. I was shocked to find how many young advisers looking to join my company were expecting to be given leads and had no idea at all how to prospect, network and develop their own clients. In this book I hope to redress the balance. We'll look at the key factors that influence a prospective client in deciding where to turn for advice. We'll cover the secrets to building lasting client relationships and in the process you'll discover that there are some really basic and straightforward things you can do to build your business one client at a time.

I'm also addressing the many thousands of financial services intermediaries in parts of the world where the products are relatively new, where prosperity and financial independence are now becoming far more achievable: countries such as Poland, Hungary, The Czech Republic, Greece and Russia along with India and the Far East.

I'm making some basic assumptions: that you are honest, technically competent in the areas in which you advise and that you hold the necessary licences and authorisation in your particular national or state jurisdiction. Above all you want to enjoy a long and happy career in this, your chosen profession, and you want highly satisfied clients who don't complain when matters beyond your control go against them.

Chapter 1
Trust: the Vital Ingredient

The late American comedian George Burns once said famously, "The most important thing in acting is honesty. If you can fake that, you've got it made!" Well, that may be true in the acting profession; we, however, are not acting, we are being ourselves. Surveys taken amongst people looking for financial advice reveal that above everything else people are looking for **an adviser they can trust.** Similarly, when discussing the aspirations of many people new to our profession they state their goal as *to be a trusted adviser*. In short, trust is placed higher on the list of credentials than almost any other factor, including qualifications. The importance of building and maintaining trust in our client relationships will be a recurring theme throughout this book. Looking at it another way, when even the most experienced and knowledgeable adviser acts against the interest of his or her client then the trust is broken, leading to the potential loss of that client or worse.

So, if trust is so important how come most of the books and almost all the emphasis in training aimed at financial service professionals focus on the technical aspects of financial planning and the associated products to the virtual exclusion of everything else? The fact is, most of the training given to advisers, along with much of the recommended reading, is prepared by the companies behind life insurance and mutual fund products, or by professional accreditation bodies who also sell technical training courses based on their technical examinations. Trust is that intangible, which only we ourselves can build, so we have only ourselves to blame if we fail to build trust, or if we damage our reputation and lose it.

Simple steps to building trust

The most important ingredient in building trust is integrity. Our integrity is the one thing we own, and which no one can take from us. Think about it: other people can steal your possessions, burn your house down, physically attack you or your family and yet no one can take your integrity from you. The only way to lose your integrity is to give it up voluntarily.

So the starting point in building trust is to always act with integrity in every aspect of your life, particularly in your business dealings.

Are you trustworthy? Take this simple test

What would your clients, business associates, family and friends say about you at your funeral? The key thing is, will what they say be in line with what you would want them to say?

In any sales-related business, goals and targets are spoken of every day, yet most of these are financial or material goals. I believe the most powerful goal is the *being goal*: to be the best we can in all aspects of our lives. Once we have a *being goal*, making decisions that affect our integrity becomes much more straightforward.

We can also go a long way towards proving our integrity through our reliability and honesty. Dan Sullivan, creator of *the Strategic Coach® Program*, says that all you have to do to stand out from everyone else is to turn up on time, do what you say, finish what you start, and say please and thank you. Isn't it ironic that being trusted can be so simple! Yet very few people do these things.

There are several other key aspects to building and maintaining trust including body language, time management, learning to listen, our image, and our ability to add value – sometimes called *going the extra mile*. The outcome of successfully building trusting relationships with our clients is that we have an outstanding reputation and our clients have absolute confidence in us. This leads naturally to personal introductions from one client to another which is universally accepted as being the most effective way to build any long-term business.

In the following chapters, you will discover more ideas for building and reinforcing trust.

Chapter 2
First Impressions

We've all heard the expression 'You never get a second chance to make a first impression'. What does this really mean though? Sociologists have come up with different thoughts on this; however it is generally accepted that people form their first opinion of us within 45 seconds to two minutes of meeting us. Importantly, that first impression will stick, so it really is important to make the most of that initial opportunity.

Creating the right first impression starts with how we appear visually, how we greet each other, the way we listen and, above all, the silent signals we send through our posture and our unconscious mannerisms - in other words our body language.

Our appearance

There are regional differences around the world; however, for business we should wear business clothes, neatly pressed and our shoes must be clean. When driving any distance to meet a client, drive in soft shoes and change into the business shoes on arrival. Men should usually wear a tie and because we will be pointing things out with our fingers, our nails should be neatly trimmed and clean. If you bite your nails then stop! I bit my nails for the first twenty years of my life until I realised that it was completely unacceptable.

Unless we are calling on farmers or travelling on unmade roads, our cars should be clean, both inside and out.

The exploding briefcase (my own first impression!)

I remember my very first sales call. I was terribly nervous and had booked an appointment with Mr Niarchos, the owner of an import export company in Southampton Row, London. Prior to this I didn't even own a briefcase so I had gone out and bought the cheapest one I could find which was made of some kind of fibre board with very cheap hinges and catches.

I arrived at the appointment and ascended the stairs hesitantly to the first floor reception where, after introducing myself, I sat nervously waiting to meet my prospect.

After what seemed like an age, I was shown into an office where Mr Niarchos sat behind a large, imposing desk. He motioned for me to sit down and with a rather worrying lack of interest asked me to explain why I was there.

I launched straight away into talking about my products. I had asked him no questions and after a few minutes he interrupted and said, "Mr Clarke I don't think I am going to be interested in anything and I'm in a bit of a hurry so I'll have to call the meeting to a close." He then stood, indicating that it was time for me to leave.

I nervously grabbed my cheap briefcase and, in my hurry to leave, the catches sprang open and the contents spilled all over the floor of his office, including my cheese and tomato sandwich, a banana and two or three sales aids. I had never felt more embarrassed!

Mr Niarchos broke into a warm smile just as his secretary entered the room and the two of them started helping me pick up the mess on the floor.

This rather embarrassing event had a happy ending. Mr Niarchos seemed to have some sympathy with my predicament and, with a smile on his face, invited me to sit down again. He then went on to explain that he really didn't think that he particularly needed my services; however, on reflection he did think that one of his close associates would probably be very interested. He picked up the telephone, made a call and booked me an appointment for later that day, down the road with his associate who did in fact become my first client!

Before I left, Mr Niarchos gave me some great advice! He recommended that I upgrade my briefcase to something a bit more suitable, suggesting that even a second hand, good-quality briefcase would be better than a cheap new one. Fortunately that part of London was (and still is) full of luggage shops and I bought a replacement briefcase later that day, after completing the second call successfully.

I can remember well some of those early meetings sitting nervously in an unfamiliar reception area, trying to make small talk with the receptionist to take my mind off my state of near panic at the prospect of another cold call. On one occasion I was chatting to a very attractive young lady in an office in Brentwood, Essex, a town where I spent much of my youth. Trying to impress her, I mentioned that I used to be in a rock 'n roll band that played in the Artichoke pub in Brentwood. When she asked me the name of the band, her response put me firmly back in my place, "Oh, yes, I know that name, my mum was one of your fans!" The meeting with her boss was even stranger as he kept reaching forward and grabbing my knee to emphasise a point. Shortly afterwards, I left that office after another unsuccessful call without even a glance at the receptionist!

A good set of wheels

I also remember the first time I realised the power of having a quality motor car. Once again it was early on in my career and my own vehicle, a very tired Ford Cortina with in excess of 100,000 miles to its credit, was being repaired. One of my friends loaned me his Mercedes delivery van which I parked in a side street before calling on my prospects, a young couple called Diane and David who came from a list of leads I'd bought. Having failed miserably with cold calls I decided to try using some qualified leads, bought from a specialist company. Without thinking about it, I tossed the vehicle keys on the coffee table as I sat down in Diane and David's living room.

The meeting went surprisingly well and much to my delight I was able to complete some business on the first meeting. With the business done, Diane offered me another cup of coffee and David seemed quite eager to chat about some of his friends who might be interested in meeting me. I asked David if there was any particular aspect of my service that he felt stood out for the purposes of setting me apart from other advisers. To my embarrassment, he responded that he felt my presentation was fairly average, however I was obviously successful or (pointing at my key ring) I wouldn't be able to afford the Mercedes! The couple in question are still clients and it was over 12 months before I decided to come clean and explain that the key ring which had so impressed David actually belonged to a Mercedes delivery van loaned to me by one of my sympathetic neighbours!

Were you there for that first impression?

For those of us who work within our own communities we need to be fully aware of how many of our future prospects might see us, hear about us or otherwise come into contact with us when we are <u>not</u> working. It's just as important that we create the right impression at all times, even when we're off duty. Now, I'm not suggesting we should spend all our time dressed up in business clothes on the off-chance that we may meet a future prospect! What I am suggesting however is that we should always conduct ourselves appropriately, be courteous to strangers, open doors for people - especially people with baby buggies or heavy shopping - drive sensibly and do nothing in our private lives which might come back to haunt us!

Quite recently I took on a new client who, I found out later, is on the committee of my local yacht club. It turned out that she knew my boat and singled me out as one of the few club members to adhere to the speed limit when navigating between the moorings. Had I been less considerate I could easily have lost that new client!

Dr Livingstone I presume? (Cultural differences)

These words were used by the American, Charles Stanley, when he discovered the English adventurer David Livingstone after three years of searching for him, whilst exploring East Africa. In his book *How I found Livingstone*, Charles Stanley writes, "I would have embraced him, only he being an Englishman, I did not know how he would receive me. So I did what cowardice and false pride suggested was the best thing – walked deliberately to him, took off my hat and said, 'Dr Livingstone I presume?'"

This simple example highlights the fact that, even in 1870, travellers were aware of the difficulties that can arise through failing to recognise the different customs that prevail when people meet and greet one another. This is particularly true today when so many of the people we are likely to meet come from different countries, different cultural backgrounds and different traditions. Yet I find it amazing that some people seem completely oblivious to the issue. Many books have been written about cultural differences between people and how to avoid social gaffes especially when travelling abroad. It pays to do some homework, particularly if we are going to meet somebody whose brain has been programmed to respond to an entirely different set of signals from our own!

I did some calculations to illustrate the importance of first impressions. I estimated I had met 25,000 people between May 1981 when I started my business to the end of 2007. I generated £6,250,000 gross fees and commissions during that period. Only around 1,000 of those original people became clients; however, based on these figures *each encounter* earned me £250. So when you think of it that way if everyone you meet, however you meet them, could be worth £250 (US$425), knowing this how much more care would we all take about the way we meet and greet people?

There is a story that in World War II some American and British soldiers working undercover in North Africa were discovered by the Germans because the Americans were sitting cross-legged showing the soles of their feet which, in that particular part of the world, no native would have done. Hearing that story was the first time that I was aware of this particular cultural essential when dealing with Arabs. I put this to good use a few years ago when I met Mr Amin, an Egyptian businessman, at the Park Lane Hotel in London. He had what seemed at the time to be a strange ritual when holding meetings in that he would invite all the various people he wanted to see at roughly the same time. We all sat across the room in a crescent formation, just far enough away from him that we couldn't hear the conversation at his table. He would then call us over individually when he wanted to speak to us.

At the end of the meeting I had no idea whether I was to be doing business with him or not until he called me to give me the go-ahead. Subsequently, I met his wife who was born in England. She confided in me that it was the way I sat whilst waiting for my turn that convinced her husband that he would be happy doing business with me!

Chapter 3
Do as you would be done by?
Not necessarily!

When Charles Kingsley wrote the famous children's storybook *The Water Babies* in 1862, he included two characters: Mrs Doasyouwouldbedoneby and Mrs Bedonebyasyoudid. The adage '*Do as you would be done by*' has remained in the English language as a first principle in how to behave with other people. These days, however, in the multicultural world in which we live, doing this could well get us into serious trouble! I suggest a more appropriate, if slightly clumsy, adage would be '*Do to others as they would have done unto themselves*'. In other words, we should do our best to find out how the people we encounter would prefer to be treated according to their own standards and culture, and then do our best to emulate this. But how? Fortunately, several tools are available to make our lives much simpler.

Transactional Analysis is the theory developed by Claude Steiner and Eric Berne, and explains why our own behaviour and beliefs are affected by that of our parents. Eric Berne went on to write the book *What Do You Do After You Say Hello?* which opens up the whole question of how people <u>love</u> to buy, whilst they actually <u>hate</u> being sold to.

There have been a number of other specialists who have developed the whole field of behavioural styles; among my favourites are Larry Wilson, Tony Alessandra and Kathy Kolbe. There is an extensive range of books, audios and videos available covering the subject in detail. Suffice it to say that enough has been written on the subject to establish that it does have a great deal of relevance and that we would do well to understand the importance of finding out how individual people prefer to do business and to do our best to meet that requirement. Resist the people who tell you it's all mumbo-jumbo. This stuff really does work!

In my own business for example, I always ask my clients how they prefer to communicate with me: by email, telephone, post or in face-to-face meetings. I have a couple of clients who always text me when they want something. This, by the way, is very much a 'Generation Y' thing and we would all do well to make sure we adapt to this most recent consumer grouping.

The most important words

The most important words to a person are his or her own name. Get that wrong and we are very much on the wrong foot. In my business we also ask our clients how they prefer to be addressed: Mr J Black and Mrs D Black, Mr and Mrs John Black, Mr and Mrs Black etc. We then do our best to meet these requirements as far as possible. Many married women now prefer to retain their maiden name and we should no longer presume that the man's name should always come first of the two. Same sex relationships and people co-habiting whilst not strictly being in a relationship also come into this. One of my pet hates is having to compromise to accommodate the shortcomings of a computer system and I changed the database system we used because it was inflexible in this respect. In fact, it's so important to get this right that in our office we still type certain things out using the clients' preferred title and name.

Using an example from the motor trade, I used to call the Mercedes Benz dealer to book a service for my car and their first question was, "What's the registration number?" Even after five years of having them collect my car I always had to explain how to find my office. In short, they had copious amounts of information about my car yet precious little about me. I pointed this out to the owner of the dealership and his answer was that the computer systems were supplied by the manufacturer in Germany and there was nowhere on the database to record this information. I suggested he would do well to invest a few pounds in a PC with a contact management system so they could start treating their customers with the same level of reverence as they appeared to show to the cars. My suggestion fell on deaf ears. I now drive a different brand of car and, perhaps more importantly, buy from a dealer with more customer focus!

Until my back-office system was good enough to do the whole job, I used to run a separate contact management system so I could record those all-important details such as wedding anniversaries, children's birthdays, religious festivals and a host of other details of far greater importance to our clients than the number of their policy. For anyone working for an insurance company where the database is almost entirely related to policy records and hard facts about the policyholder, I highly recommend doing this. Most contact management systems such as Goldmine and ACT! are incredibly good value and help you store and retrieve really impressive relationship management information.

In the UK, financial advisers are using psychometric testing increasingly to assist in evaluating the investment risk profile of their clients. I have used psychometrics in one form or another since I was first introduced to the technique in 1981, mostly with employees but also on occasions with clients, to help identify how best to communicate with them. There are many companies now offering online tests based on the DISC (Dominance, Influence, Steadiness and Compliance) system at a very reasonable charge. For people not familiar with this I recommended doing some research. In its most basic form the system divides us all into one of four predominant types as in the table below.

Analytical	Driver
Amiable	Expressive

To me the most important piece of information I discovered is that whilst we will all get on pretty well with most people, we are more likely to get on extremely well with people in our own corner of this chart and we will have the greatest difficulty relating to people diagonally opposite us.

Being someone who prefers to get to the point when learning something, I decided that the starting point for me would be to understand how better to get on with people <u>least</u> like me which, in my case, meant I had to learn how to deal better with Analyticals. These people are often found in accountancy and law; as these are very important professionals to get to know, an understanding of how they like to do business turned out to be a great deal more useful than I could have hoped. Many of the financial advisers I meet in the UK these days, especially the younger ones, are Analyticals and really do need to understand the other three styles as they will have the greatest difficulty relating to other types of people.

The starting point for me was to learn to recognise the different personality styles by observing the three most significant externally-detectable indicators:

- the way people behaved in the first few minutes of meeting them

- the way they organise their offices and homes

- the way they speak.

An investment in this particular area of knowledge can transform our business relationships and is a further step towards increasing the chances of doing business with over 75% of the people we meet.

If we can obtain an understanding of behavioural styles and become a master of the art of dealing with people *on their terms,* we are well on the way to being able to deal with difficult people, gain cooperation from people with whom we come into contact and positively influence those about us. There are some useful references in the appendix at the end of the book.

Chapter 4
So tell me what you want, what you really, really want!

The theme of the Spice Girls' first hit record was *Tell me what you want* not *Tell me what you need*! We can make great leaps forward in our business by talking to our clients and prospects about **what they want** rather than **what they need**. Of course, this goes directly against the basic training that most of us receive when we start in business where, even today in the 21st Century, much of the training is based on a 'needs analysis'.

When we talk to people about their needs, we have to **sell** to them whereas when we ask them what they want, we are **helping them to buy**. This is a far simpler and more enjoyable process both for us and for our clients. We also reap greater rewards, as *wants* are almost always larger and more exiting than mere *needs*.

In the financial services business we are almost always dealing with the future. When we invest money on behalf of clients we are investing for the medium to long term, and when we arrange life insurance the proceeds are usually designed to be delivered well into the future. Likewise with retirement planning.

We should tell our clients they have time to design the future they want and show them that with our help they can achieve it! In my experience, many clients have yet to appreciate that they can plan a certain future for themselves and their families should they really want to.

Talking about wants rather than needs also helps us in building lasting relationships with our clients. They see us as someone on their side helping them get what they want. Because of this they are also more likely to refer us to their friends and colleagues. Always ask a client to reconfirm, "Is that what you want?" especially whenever you hear them say, "I think I need..."

Sometimes, asking people what they want can also help us flush out a timewaster. I remember once talking to a business owner about what his wife and family would do if he were to die prematurely. He said that they would have to sell the house and move in with her mother. I asked him if that's what he wanted to happen and he said it certainly was, he wouldn't be wasting any money when his mother-in-law had a big house and was quite capable of looking after the family. Needless to say I wasted no more time with that prospect! (Mind you, looking back I should probably have asked for an introduction to his mother-in-law!)

I firmly believe it is not our job to tell clients what they should or should not do in the matter of family succession. We should find out what they want to happen and then make sure their financial and legal arrangements will facilitate this. If there are any gaps or inappropriate planning it is our role to point this out and offer the appropriate solution. For example, in the UK it is customary for families to arrange their legal affairs through will planning so as to minimise estate taxes (Inheritance Tax). This may not suit everyone, however, especially those whose religious or cultural beliefs lead them toward a different path. So it pays to understand how a Muslim or a Hindu, for example, may prefer to arrange things. Sometimes this will result in a higher amount of Inheritance Tax, however that's where life insurance can come to the rescue. I've arranged several very large life policies to pay the resulting additional death taxes arising in the UK when a man decides to leave much of his estate to his children and only part to his spouse.

I have several lawyers among my contacts who know, for example, how to draw up a Sharia will.

Discussing the sensitive issue of death and family succession can sometimes reveal unexpected questions. I'd been dealing with a lovely Indian couple for some years and they were approaching retirement. They had two children and I wanted to make sure they were happy with what would happen in the event of the death of either parent.

The wife asked me, "Lee, can we ask you a sensitive question?"

"Of course," I replied.

"In order for our children to get a death certificate when we die, does there have to be a dead body?" I resisted a natural impulse to make some kind of humorous comment and responded, "Well, it is usually a requirement, why do you ask?" She went on to explain that in their religion they believed when their time came they would just disappear and arrive in Heaven, leaving no material body behind. I simply explained that if that happened the law would require a period of seven years to elapse before they could be certified as dead, during which time their assets would be frozen and could not be passed to the children.

This resulted in the clients placing money into Trust and then in a special investment vehicle to fund for the upkeep of their assets (house, cars etc.) during that seven-year period. So, whereas a cynical laugh at their question would probably have lost me the clients, my approach resulted in extra business!

Much more recently, a business owner and client of mine named Stan presented me with a financial planning report put together on a fee basis by another adviser. "This report says that I need £100,000 more life insurance, what do you think?" asked Stan. As you can imagine, I was somewhat dismayed that he had been talking to someone else; however, Stan read my mind and told me to relax. "Lee," he said, "You'd have got someone in your office to push all these numbers though a computer program and come out with a similar report so I just got the job done for you. Tell me what you think." I ran through the report and I admitted that many of the ideas in the report were sound and, indeed, Stan was the first to accept that there was nothing new in the report that I'd not already drawn to his attention. I did however point out that I felt the amount of life insurance suggested was woefully inadequate. Typical of many such reports, the life insurance requirement had been calculated by reference to Stan's debts and had significantly understated the lifestyle requirements of the family in the event of his death. *Needs*, rather than *wants*. I asked Stan what he was working towards with his business. He explained that, over the next five years, he expected to be able to sell his business for several million pounds, which would clear all his debts and enable him and his family to live comfortably without the need to work again. I asked him what he meant by 'comfortably', and he said that he was planning to finish the building of his five-bedroomed home, that he wanted a couple of investment properties to produce income and that, above all, he wanted to be able to travel and enjoy life with his wife Peggy who, up to now, had been working six days a week in the office.

I asked him to explain further the type of travel he wanted to do, we worked on the income this would require and it was quite clear that for Stan to achieve this he was going to need to build an asset base of several million pounds in order to provide the income and lifestyle he wanted for his family.

I pointed out there was a weakness in Stan's planning in that, provided he kept on working, he would probably achieve his goals. He had significant ambition, vision and plenty of energy but the weakness was that if Stan didn't make it the plans would fail. As long as he was able to complete his projects over the next five years, he would probably achieve his goals but if he were to die in the attempt, they would fall significantly short. I asked him, therefore, if he wanted his wife and family to be able to enjoy the lifestyle he was creating for them even if he was unfortunate enough to die before this was completed. He said that this was certainly what he wanted.

This resulted in the sale of the largest life insurance policy I had sold up to that date; however the story wasn't over. When the medical underwriting was carried out it transpired that Stan had a significant number of health problems which, when added together, resulted in a substantial loading of the premium. In fact, the amount of money that the insurance company wanted was more than Stan's total monthly income!

Fortunately, because I had gone through the process of discussing what Stan wanted, rather than what he *needed,* he knew that he had to find the money from somewhere and, in line with what many business owners do, he found some more money from within the business cash flow and was able to cover the premiums. He still felt, however, that such a large monthly commitment should be undertaken with the full agreement of his family and so he told me he was going to discuss it with them over the weekend. For me this was an extremely long weekend as I waited with bated breath for Stan's call the following Monday.

When Stan finally rang me at 4.30 pm the next Monday, he told me that he'd run through much the same discussion with his wife and children as I had gone though with him, and they realised that this substantial life insurance policy was vital to their financial well-being and readily agreed that he should pay the premiums.

This is a really good example of dealing with wants rather than needs and shows how our clients really want to buy when they can see this it as something that will help them achieve what they want.

Chapter 5
Using Positive Language

When helping prospects to think about what they want, use positive language rather than negative. There's a fair bit of psychology in this. We are told the conscious mind can only hold one thought at a time. Introduce a ***positive*** thought and it will boot out any ***negative*** thought that might be lingering there. Our brain is also extremely clever in that it has a self-seeking mechanism built in to help us achieve our goals. This is part of the Law of Attraction, highlighted in Rhonda Byrne's successful book *The Secret*. If you have not read it, you should! Most of our clients are unaware of the self-seeking nature of the brain and when we talk to them about what they want they may well say something like, "In an ideal world......but....." Helping our clients to think bigger thoughts, dream bigger dreams and ultimately achieve greater things in life is one of the privileges of our profession – oh, and it pays very well too! Bigger dreams need bigger plans and our clients will never stray once they have discussed their dreams and ambitions with us. I give copies of *The Secret* to clients who need some encouragement with setting challenging goals.

When writing to our clients we must be sure to continue using positive words. How many letters have you seen which end with 'If you have any queries please do not hesitate to contact me.' Try 'Please contact me with any queries' - not only is this shorter, it's far more positive and, once again, a bit of psychology is involved. The brain has problems dealing with negative instructions and tends to screen out 'do not', just leaving 'hesitate to contact me.' Have you ever wondered why so few people do contact you? In the UK, signs that order 'Do Not Walk on the Grass' are largely ignored, whereas signs requesting 'Keep off the Grass' are normally obeyed. I often wonder why at airports they keep telling us, "Do not leave your baggage unattended," whereas perhaps they should be saying, "Keep your baggage with you at all times."

Using positive language can be useful at home too! In my case, my wife used to say to me in the morning when I came down for breakfast, "Don't forget to bring your empty coffee mug with you." Needless to say, I used to arrive in the kitchen without it. Changing her words to "Please bring your coffee cup when you come downstairs," was all it took to make sure I almost always remembered!

Using the present tense

In our own lives, we should always use the present tense when setting goals to achieve what we want. In the simplest example, saying to ourselves, "I am a successful financial adviser" will bring us closer to that reality much faster than saying, "One day I want to be a successful financial adviser." If we teach these present tense ideas to our clients, they will see their own goals coming to fruition far more quickly and they will see us as a genuinely positive influence in their lives. Let's show our clients how to achieve their goals. Where we can see that something - or someone - could help our clients we should try to introduce them. There's more about Networking later in the book.

Today language

When our clients have difficulty accepting that they will die one day, say to them, "Imagine that I'm sitting here today with your widow and that you had died last night. What would you like me to be able to tell your widow this morning?" This will really focus your client's thinking on the situation. This is not some event that *may* happen at some distant point in the future - it's now, today, and our clients have to visualise this.

Chapter 6
The Three Key Stages in Professional Development

People want our expertise and our wisdom, not just information

These days no one is short of information. People are deluged with information in leaflets, on the Internet, on television and radio and in general advertising. What people want is to know **what to do with the information**! I believe there are three stages to our own professional learning.

1. Gaining knowledge

2. Gaining experience

3. Gaining wisdom

Experience comes after we've dealt with many actual cases. Information we obtain is evaluated and the appropriate recommendation given based on the specific situation of a particular client.

Wisdom is the final stage and, more often than not, helps us decide when NOT to implement what experience would normally tell us is the correct advice. There's no fast-track to wisdom, only time; many real-life client experiences will bring us wisdom.

Janet and Simon, for example, had been introduced by Chris who was Simon's boss and also one of my clients. A young couple of 21 and 19, they came to see me shortly before they got married. They were buying their first home and between the two of them they had three lever-arch files full of clippings from magazines about mortgages, life insurance, savings and so forth. They were thoroughly confused.

I asked them what they knew about me and what they wanted to get from our meeting. They told me that, based on the introduction from Chris, they understood that I could be trusted to tell them what they should do. (Remember that at the beginning of the book I mentioned that there would be frequent references to trust!)

Janet and Simon were planning to get married in about a year's time. I told them precisely what they should do and we put together a plan. Many years later, the couple are now aged 40 and have three children. They are still clients, although sadly their marriage ended in divorce a few years ago and each has now remarried. Simon bought a business with a new business partner, who is also now a client and we put in place a pension scheme for their fifty employees.

Simon's partner has taken advice from me and we have set up a Trust for his disabled daughter. Several of the employees in their business have become individual clients while numerous other financial advisers have prospected my client and his company unsuccessfully. I had dinner recently with Simon and his wife and we were reflecting on the last twenty years. Simon told me that my willingness to give general advice and to be available as a sounding board, even when no immediate business would result, was one of the primary reasons that they trusted me and have never allowed anyone else to challenge my advice.

This case illustrates perfectly the value our clients put on having a trusted adviser and, in the context of this book, how being a trusted adviser is the secret to what I call 'The Magic of Compound Interest in Relationships' when building a business.

Our compliance departments and our regulators will stipulate all sorts of information that we have to give to our clients at the point of sale. In my experience, however, the most important sale is made when our prospect first decides to ask us for advice. To lose the business after getting to that stage we have to do something wrong.

Coming back to integrity and trust, as long as we give our clients the right advice for their circumstances, even if it is that they should do nothing at this immediate moment, we will retain their trust and our own integrity and, when the time is right, business will be done.

Chapter 7
Respect for our Competitors

In the 'dog eat dog' world in which we seem to live these days I firmly believe that we have to stand apart from people who try and gain advantage at the expense of someone else's reputation. In fact, demonstrating respect for your competitors can seriously improve your wealth! In the 1980s I met John Smith who had a business in industrial photography with another of my clients. I had only recently been advised by one of my successful friends that I should always be ready to be 'first reserve' when meeting somebody who already had an established relationship with a financial adviser. Another of my basic principles came in here: never to criticise or undermine a financial adviser who has a good relationship with my prospect. I don't appreciate it when it happens to me so I don't do it; sometimes I think about doing it but my principle is firm. It's too easy to find fault with another professional's advice. As my good friend Richard Bateman says, "If you have two dentists you'll end up with no teeth!" I had already established that John seemed to have been well provided for with the advice he had received from his long-standing adviser and (as it turned out) good friend. So I suggested that he continue to follow his friend's advice but that I would always be happy to assist if at some point in time that advice was no longer available. So I'd created my 'first reserve' position.

It was five years later when John Smith called me to say that he was taking early retirement and that he had an Open Market Option (the right to transfer the accumulated retirement fund to any other insurer offering better annuity rates) under the terms of his pension scheme. His regular adviser had told him that his company did not do a particularly thorough job with these Open Market Options and that it might be an idea for him to contact me, given that I had always offered to provide advice if and when it was needed. I leapt at the opportunity to assist John, who was only 53 at the time. For two more years his adviser continued to look after his other financial needs, however he soon retired and I stepped in. I am pleased to say that I have been advising John ever since, most recently helping him with further retirement options as he approached his 75th birthday!

A particularly nice twist in this story is that when John's original financial adviser eventually decided to retire, he too came to me for advice with his own Open Market Option for the same reasons.

John has since introduced me to his two sons, both of whom have become clients. One of the sons is now a director of a large engineering company and we have recently established a pension scheme for the 57 employees of that company.

I am really saddened by the fact that the Code of Conduct of my primary professional body in the UK makes no reference at all to showing respect for fellow members. In fact one gets to Rule 14 before there's anything about conduct towards clients!

Chapter 8
A Bicycle made for Two

Usually our family clients mostly want the same major things in life although in my entire career I've only come across two people who actually owned a tandem (a bicycle made for two). So, when talking to a couple, it is important to make sure we establish the wants of both parties. In the first few years of my career, there were many occasions when I lost the business but couldn't work out why. Discussing the case with my more experienced colleagues it became clear that whilst the husband, for example, was nodding enthusiastically about my proposals, his wife was giving strong body language signals that she was not so keen! When dealing with people's wants, we need to make sure we clarify the position with both parties. In fact, when dealing with personal financial planning, ideally we should insist on presenting to both partners at the same time.

When I first met Brian he was not particularly keen to see me. He'd been dealing with another financial adviser and thought he had all he needed. To complicate matters further, the other adviser was well-established and also introduced business to Brian on a regular basis. My only asset was that I knew my stuff. I suspected the other adviser had relied on his friendship with Brian to keep others at bay. Fortunately, Brian's wife Yvonne had been working for me as a part-time secretary and she felt he should at least give me an opportunity to explain what I could do for him. With Brian's agreement I was invited to dinner one evening. When I met him, Brian had paid just £500 into his pension fund, paid in as a lump sum two years previously through the other financial adviser.

Rather than criticise the other adviser for not doing enough, I complimented Brian on the start he'd made on his financial planning. Had I criticised the other adviser I would, by implication, have been criticising Brian. Never do this and always compliment people on whatever they've done so far with their finances, however small. After all, a journey of a thousand miles begins with a single step!

Brian was mainly interested in money-making ideas and was quite resistant to my suggestions that he should have some life insurance and critical illness cover. It was easy to see how the other adviser had simply appealed to the soft side of Brian's financial thinking whilst treating the idea of life and critical illness insurance as a no-go area. I put forward some logical arguments to Brian and Yvonne and eventually Brian agreed to my recommendations. He also started putting some money into his retirement fund on a regular basis.

Over the years Brian had a number of accountants. None of the earlier ones was pro-active in giving tax-saving advice so I often found myself having to stand by and watch while the accountant implemented some of my suggestions for saving tax, charging Brian for this while I got nothing. In time, however, Brian did notice this and on one occasion when we were going to dinner with his current accountant he said to me in a discreet aside, "Lee you know I have lost count of the number of times I have acted on your advice on a tax-saving matter only to see my accountant charge me for implementing the advice while you have appeared to get nothing from it. How do you feel about this?" I was able to point out to Brian that whilst his accountants had come and gone I was still there and that he had introduced me to a number of his family and friends and I certainly wasn't complaining!

As time went by, Brian and Yvonne's children grew up and two of them became clients of mine. It was one of their daughters who called me to say she was very concerned about Brian who had been round to her house in quite a distressed state. Brian had always been extremely fit. I had played the occasional game of squash with him and he always beat me; Brian was very competitive in everything he did. More recently, however, his health had deteriorated somewhat; he had always suffered from asthma but this was something else. It transpired after a medical investigation that Brian had developed Angina and this led to him having Angioplasty which qualified him for a claim on his critical illness policy.

Brian told me that the payout for the policy meant that he would not have to go back to work and that he could plan to retire two years earlier than he had intended to. I thought back to the time just twelve years earlier when Brian had been so resistant to the idea of critical illness insurance when he was beating me regularly on the squash court and I felt pleased that I had persisted and that he had taken my advice.

Brian had also continued to fund his retirement plan and in recent years he had been putting in as much as the Inland Revenue would allow. Coupled with some investments in property, Brian's financial future was assured.

The key point about this story is that being professional, knowing our stuff and being prepared to tell people things they may prefer not to hear can pay off. The story also validates the importance of engaging both husband and wife in the process.

Chapter 9
Finding the Money:
understanding accounts

I related the story in Chapter 4 about Stan - how he knew he had to find the money from somewhere in his business to pay the premiums. I strongly recommend that we learn how to help our clients find the money! In all the years I have been in this business, I've met people with hardly any money and people whose wealth runs into many millions, and yet I've never met anyone with 'spare' money!

The fact is no one has any spare money, it is almost all fully allocated and, even if it is not, people rarely know where their money goes and I am sure we've all met people who still have some month left at the end of their money!

Many years ago I asked my accountant to teach me the basics of reading a set of company accounts. Fortunately, all limited companies in the UK have to file their accounts at Companies House where the records are available to the public. Before talking to a new business-owner client, I print off a set of the most recent accounts from the Companies House website, and there's almost always an opportunity to save some money somewhere in those accounts.

When dealing with an existing client, I will always ask them to let me have an advance copy of their most recent accounts before an annual review meeting and, even better, where I have managed to build a relationship with my client's accountant, I always arrange for the accountant to make these available to me without bothering the client. This way, the client regards both the accountant and myself in a better light, seeing us as working as part of a team, rather than in opposition to one another as is so often the case.

In a domestic situation we also need to know how to help our clients find the money. Many people tell me they have no idea where their money goes and that at best they can account for only half their monthly expenditure. A really good idea is to give these clients a little notebook and ask them to record everything they spend for the following month. Every magazine, newspaper, item of clothing, food and so on. I actually did this myself a few years back and I was staggered at the wasted money. In every case where I've used this idea clients who are serious about saving expenditure report saving between 15% and 25% of their monthly income. That's an amazing figure and it goes to show that when people decide to prioritise their financial planning they can find the money with our help.

Of course, it doesn't always work. One of my clients who was also a very old friend had asked for my help. It was clear that, whilst he had a good lifestyle at the time, he would be significantly short of money in retirement, which was only ten years away (120 pay days!) I tried to get together with him on several occasions and each time he would say, "We can't do Thursday, that's our Spanish lesson and Tuesdays we go horse riding" - things like that. I pointed out that if he didn't get his finances straight the Spanish lessons would be a waste of time and money as he wouldn't be able to afford the holidays. Likewise why not trade one riding lesson for a meeting that might make it possible to keep riding when they retired?

We got some planning in place, however his career took a turn for the worse and it was his pension contributions, not the riding lessons, that he cancelled. This was not the first time he'd acted this way so I told him that, sadly, I could no longer have him as a client if whenever he felt under any kind of financial pressure it was his financial planning rather than his leisure activities that he cancelled.

Another client who knew me quite well and who seriously needed to build up his savings and retirement funds invited me to stay the night as they lived three hours away from me. I brought a bottle of wine as a contribution to our evening meal. My client thanked me and said, "We're taking you out to dinner. Mary doesn't cook during the week." I chose my moment carefully to suggest that maybe Mary *should* cook during the week and that meals out should be an occasional treat or they might never be able to retire.

John was a golfer and had asked for retirement planning advice. He was going to be seriously short of income in retirement. He was contributing less than 2% of his earnings to retirement plans, yet he played golf three times a week. His golf club membership fee exceeded his annual pension contributions and the green fees at other clubs added even more to his outgoings. I asked him whether he expected to play more or less golf when he retired; he confirmed that he expected to play more. I suggested that unless he reduced the amount of golf now and increased his pension contributions he would have to give up golf altogether! Fortunately he took my advice and, now retired, he still plays three times a week - something, which he still reminds me, is due to my sound advice.

"I gave you two ears and one mouth!
Please use them in that proportion!"

Chapter 10
Are you listening?

There's an old adage *'God gave us two ears and one mouth and we should learn to use them in that proportion'*. In Chapter 1 when talking about trust, I mentioned how important it is to be a good listener. Listening, however, is not just about hearing! During a conversation the other party is watching us and our body language, our eyes, what we are doing with our hands and they perceive whether we are listening or not. In other words, we can hear what they are saying but are we really listening?

There are differences between men and women in casual conversation in that women can often carry on a number of conversations at once or can 'multi-task', whereas men are usually only able to do one thing at a time. Nevertheless, in a client meeting both parties should be focusing 100% on the conversation.

So starting from the perspective that we must make sure our client or prospect believes we are listening, we should adopt an interested posture. That means maintaining eye contact with our prospects whilst they are speaking, keeping our hands still and, above all, not interrupting! Listen to a TV news reporter interviewing someone. Notice that they NEVER interrupt or comment on an answer, they just go on to clarify or to ask another question. We can learn from this technique.

Visiting a very successful financial adviser a few years ago, he mentioned how surprised he was that he had not done business with the clients who had just left. His wife, who is also his PA, was standing beside us and offered the following revealing insight: "Ralph, you lost them within thirty seconds of their arrival." Non-plussed, he asked her to explain. "When they arrived you asked them how they were," she began. "Well, not that good," they responded. "Our daughter Megan's baby was stillborn and John's been made redundant," they added.

Ralph's wife continued, "Your response was, 'Oh, great! Come on in, I've got some great ideas for you!'"

Clearly Ralph had been so preoccupied with what he hoped to sell them, he had not been listening at all and had lost the sale as soon as he opened his mouth.

Chapter 11
A Meeting of Minds:
the Preliminary Discussion

Taking notes

Most people want to take notes during a meeting with their client; on the first meeting with a new prospect it is important to show respect by asking if it's OK if we make a few notes. We need to listen not only with our ears for the answer, we need to listen with our eyes! In other words, look for any signs of negative body language given by our prospect to any question, including the one asking if we can take notes. If you are in any doubt, do clarify with your prospect that the notes are for your personal use only at this stage and that your discussion will remain confidential. I've sat in on at least two interviews when the prospect answered 'No' to the question and yet the adviser simply ignored the answer and went on taking notes! This really is important, especially at such an early stage in the process.

It's important to differentiate between the notes taken during a preliminary discussion like this and the completion of a fact find which should come later, once we have agreed with our prospect that business should proceed to the next stage.

Remember we are still building trust at this stage. Think for a moment about the times in your life when a relative stranger has pulled out a form and started completing it in front of you. For example, someone coming to your home to discuss a product or service. How did you feel? What was your perception of the purpose of the form and what would happen to it? I bet that, like me, you expected the form to be sent off to his office for some purpose or other and probably to be loaded on to a database. Would you freely give private and personal information under such circumstances? We should not presume that people would freely give us the information we need to do our job when we have barely started our first meeting. The completion of a detailed fact find should only proceed once our prospect is fully relaxed and has already given some indication that business is likely to follow.

I was discussing this very point in Poland recently where I was speaking at a conference. The members of the audience were all born at a time when Poland was a communist country. People were taught from an early age to trust no one, that their neighbours and work colleagues could be spying on them and feeding information back to the secret police and so on. How much more difficult it is for them to get any information out of their clients, most of whom grew up under such difficult circumstances. Establishing a trusting relationship with their prospects and clients is absolutely paramount if they are to be able to perform their function as a financial adviser.

A while ago I said that you should sit still and not fiddle with your fingers, so what about taking notes? Well, just don't write things down while your prospect is actually speaking; wait for them to pause and then make a note. You can always fill in the gaps later, when the meeting is over and while the discussion is fresh in your mind.

Asking the right questions

Ask open questions. This means asking questions that cannot simply be answered with the words 'yes' or 'no'. The famous author, Rudyard Kipling wrote:

"I have six honest serving men,

They taught me all I knew,

Their names are What, and Why, and How,

and Where and When and Who."

These words are powerful in asking open questions because our prospect or client has to answer with a considered reply. They cannot simply respond 'yes' or 'no'.

One word of warning, however: be very careful using the word *why*? The reason for this is that it can be seen as a very challenging word and whilst there are appropriate places to ask 'Why?', it's very important to avoid such a challenging question early on in our relationship with our client or prospect. I said "don't interrupt", so if something comes up during the reply to your question which you feel needs to be clarified, make a very brief note, maybe just one word, and then raise the question when your prospect has finished speaking.

We can usually tell if it's been a successful meeting by who has done the most talking. The person speaking is usually the one having the most fun, so if our prospect or client is doing most of the speaking we're on the right track!

I remember an incident a few years ago which really demonstrated the power of allowing your prospect to do most of the talking. I had been given twenty minutes to introduce myself and make a brief pitch for some business with a prospect who had already told me that he was unlikely to do the business with me as he had met several other financial advisers and had more or less made up his mind to do business with somebody else. The fact that we had been introduced by a mutual friend meant that he was prepared to give me a few minutes of his time.

Undeterred, I went to the meeting and, after introducing myself, I asked him an open question, "Tell me Alan, how did you get started in this business?" Well, he spoke for ten or twelve minutes non-stop before asking me if there was anything else I wanted to know. I pointed out that there were only a few minutes left of our allocated time and he told me not to worry about that. So I asked him, "So, Alan, what excites you most about your business today?" He then went on for another ten or twelve minutes telling me enthusiastically about his new product range, his competitive edge, how much he enjoyed meeting his customers and so forth. By the time he had finished, nearly 30 minutes had elapsed and he could see that I was looking a little bit concerned about the time. At that point, Alan said to me, "Well, thank you very much Lee for coming in to see me, I think that you are just the type of financial adviser I'm looking for, how do I sign up?" During the meeting I had told him almost nothing about myself; all I had done was ask him open questions about him and his business. In his mind this had been a really successful meeting! The most important sale had been made, he had decided to do business with me and price had not even been discussed!

Chapter 12
The Fact Find

I get into trouble with a lot of compliance people about completing fact finds because, coming back to the subject of listening and getting our clients to talk, there was another adage I was taught some years ago: '*Nothing stills the moving tongue more than the moving pencil!*' In most parts of the world these days, either our companies or our regulatory authorities require us to demonstrate we have all the necessary information about our client to enable us to give the right advice by completing a fact find form. Fact finds usually contain 'hard facts' such as name, date of birth, name of children, address, value of assets, amount of salary and so forth. This may help in determining somebody's needs; however, referring back to Chapter 3 we are dealing with people's **wants**. To discover someone's wants we have to look for the 'soft facts' and it's the soft facts that will help us determine the best way to help our clients achieve their wants. Soft facts include, above everything else, *how our clients feel* about things, their views and opinions, what's important to them and so forth. There's very little room on the majority of the fact finds I've seen for any of this information. The hard facts on the other hand are relatively easy to obtain later on, when the client has made a definite decision to do business with us.

Dealing with a supervised meeting

Sometimes we are expected to conduct a client meeting with a supervisor or manager present. This can be most unsettling for our client and must be handled diplomatically. I remember taking a client to meet a lawyer who was to arrange a will. My client was already feeling stressed at the prospect of discussing personal matters with a stranger, but I had said that I would be there and would assist in the event of any difficult questions. Neither my client nor I was prepared, however, when the lawyer simply announced that his para-legal trainee would be sitting in on the meeting. It completely threw my client and, as a result, the lawyer lost the business. How much better it would have been had the lawyer asked in advance if this would be acceptable, giving any necessary assurances about confidentiality and so forth. My client could have said 'No', or more likely he would have said 'Yes' - the point being it would have prepared the ground.

I find I have to explain this quite frequently, many people seemingly unaware it can cause a problem. The fact is, most people we meet have been personally introduced to us. Our prospective client has agreed to see us because the person referring them to us says we're trustworthy, competent and that we treat personal information with complete confidentiality. People do not automatically assume the same trust can be given to others who may unexpectedly be present at the meeting. Where no trust exists because the meeting is the result of a cold call then a third party in the meeting could make things even harder, as we have to sell not only our own credibility and trustworthiness but also that of others who may or may not be deserving of that trust.

When we have to have someone else present at a client meeting we should make sure the client agrees in advance and, if at all possible, avoid a supervised meeting where we know the client or prospect has some sensitive issue to discuss (divorce, financial problems etc). Another tip: whenever I've had to allow someone to sit in on a client meeting I ask the individual to let me explain his or her presence on the basis that we are going to see another client together, so hopefully it will be OK if my colleague comes in with me to the meeting. This is usually true, as my compliance colleague or sales manager is probably with me all day and we would probably be seeing more than one client. However, by explaining it this way I avoid the client thinking someone is checking up on me. I make sure I bring my supervisor in on the discussion from time to time, by saying something like, "…don't you agree, Alan?" or "Had you any other thoughts, Alan?" I can assure you that supervisors almost never want to interfere with the advice process so their silence at this point simply adds authority to the advice we've just given.

It's not easy for people new to the business to handle a supervised meeting in this way, however I strongly suggest that if you are put in the position of having to deal with an accompanied meeting, do have a discussion with your supervisor and try to agree to proceed as mentioned here.

Chapter 13
Time Management

What would you do with a three-day week? Some thoughts on time-management

In December 1973 during an extended labour dispute between the British Government and the Trade Unions, the whole of the UK was put on to a three-day working week. There was a joke going around the life insurance industry at the time:

Question: "What would you do if you were forced to work a three-day week?" Reply: "I wouldn't know what to do with the extra day!"

Seriously however, many of us take far longer to do what needs to be done, we spend a lot of time doing things that don't need to be done and generally working ineffectively. I mentioned earlier that Dan Sullivan, creator of *the Strategic Coach® Program*, says there are only four things we have to do to be successful: show up on time, do what we say, finish what we start, and say please and thank you. Turning up on time is one of the most important things in creating the right impression, building confidence in your service and ultimately becoming a trusted adviser. Sure, there are occasions when through circumstance beyond our control this is impossible. How many times, however, have I heard people say, "My train was late" or, "The traffic's always terrible getting into London at that time of day." Frankly, my answer to that is, "get an earlier train or leave home earlier"! There's simply no point in presuming that public transport will run on time, or that on the day we are travelling by car the usual traffic will mysteriously disappear and give us a clear run. Some of the most successful people I know have their days scheduled in 15-minute time slots and if we want these people as clients we really have to be on time for meetings.

Egged on...

I remember having an appointment in Leicester some two hours drive from home, at 9.00 am one morning. I was living near Swindon in the south of England at the time and decided to leave early and drive on the old Roman road known as the Fosse Way. At the Leicester end of the Fosse Way there's a small truck stop where there used to be a caravan selling tea and bacon sandwiches. I arrived there about 8.00 am, in plenty of time for my appointment an hour later. I ordered a mug of tea and decided to have the full works with an egg, bacon and tomato ketchup sandwich. As I bit into the sandwich, egg yolk and tomato ketchup squirted out all over my shirt and tie! This was not something I could rectify with a damp cloth, I had to buy a new shirt and tie. Fortunately my jacket was still hanging on a hook inside my car. I found a supermarket on the outskirts of Leicester and bought a white shirt and a tie, and changed into them in readiness for my meeting. The shirt collar was half a size too small and I can tell you that by the end of the meeting I was nearly choking. This was not the first time I'd had a disaster early in the morning.

A few years earlier I had been driving to Stoke on Trent, approximately 150 miles from my home, for an early morning meeting, leaving home in the dark. An hour into my journey, the sun was coming up and for some reason that I still can't fathom, I found myself looking down at my shoes to find I was wearing one black shoe and one brown one! I couldn't make up my mind whether to buy a tin of black shoe polish to try and make the brown shoe black, as both the shoes were of an identical design; whether to turn up as I was; or whether to buy some new shoes. Once again this was the first meeting with a new prospect so I chose option three: the new shoes! Fortunately I'd allowed myself plenty of time and I did manage to get myself a good pair of shoes. Interestingly, the person in the shoe store said I was the third person he'd met since starting to sell shoes a year ago who had had exactly the same experience as me!

Managing activity

People who know me are well aware that I am hopeless at time management. In fact the truth is we can't manage time, we can only manage the activity that we carry out within the time. Wherever we live on the globe there are twenty-four hours in a day, and 60 minutes in every hour. Fortunately, working in the financial services profession we are able to decide when we are working and when we are not working and what activities we carry out at various times of the day. I've found that grouping activities together on certain days produces the best results for me. This means that I set time aside just for making outbound telephone calls, which I do on an ex-directory line. If we are working from an office we can ask people to take messages for us while we're making outbound calls and we can return the incoming calls later. This means we can work through a list of calls until we either complete the list or we reach the end of the time allocated for doing this type of work.

I believe the most important dates we should put in our diary as far ahead as possible are the days we're not working, such as our holidays and family time. Especially towards the beginning of our career, or when we are going through a quiet period, it's very tempting to think we should prioritise business appointments and keep our diaries clear for any opportunity to meet a prospect or client. The fact is, however, our prospects and clients expect us to be busy and whilst they might ask to see us at a moment's notice, they would normally be quite surprised if we were able to do so. There's nothing wrong in being busy or having to offer an alternative date or time because you have a prior commitment.

It's all about positioning; even if we know that at the moment we're not as successful as we intend to be, we need to create the aura of being very successful and very much in demand. In fact when we appear to be at least as busy if not busier than our prospect, we will gain even more respect.

It does help to have an extremely good personal assistant. Early in my career I had to share my assistant with a number of other people, however I acted as though she was mine and mine alone, and I bought her a training video about dealing with people on the telephone. I was careful not to suggest that she was in any way inadequate in this area and that the purpose of giving her the video was to help make her life easier. Her telephone-answering skills improved quite quickly and my clients often used to comment on how pleasant she was to deal with. I now have my own extremely competent and friendly assistant and the only problem I have is that my clients would much rather talk to her than to me!

Decide which days of the week you are prepared to work in the evening (if at all) and what times in the day you prepared to have appointments. When you telephone your doctor, lawyer or accountant for an appointment, they will usually offer you a choice of appointment times or ask you if you want the next available appointment. Whatever that time is, you will have to agree to it or opt for one of the alternatives. We should be no different. Some of our clients will want to see us early in the morning, and yet we may like to have breakfast with our family. There's nothing wrong with that. Simply block out certain days of the week when you are going to definitely have breakfast with your family, and that will leave you with two or three mornings that you can make available for breakfast meetings with clients. Your family will appreciate your commitment to them and clients will also be perfectly happy with this arrangement.

Make sure you have a lunch break every day, and feel free to share that lunch with another colleague, a professional connection such as an accountant or a lawyer maybe once or twice a week. You can share information and knowledge with other professionals so you learn something from them and they learn something from you. They will appreciate it, and you will increase your knowledge and therefore the value that you bring to any of your client meetings.

Likewise when we are spending time with our families we should not be working! When we give our clients the impression that we are available all hours of the day and night by mobile phone or email, we create an unnecessary problem. They also think we are completely crazy!

Chapter 14
Agendas

Following on from some basic principles of time management discussed in Chapter 13, I suggest we should prepare an agenda for every client meeting. If we are meeting a business owner, it goes down extremely well. When meeting an existing client, email your agenda and ask them if there is anything they would like to add and then email it back to you.

When the meeting starts, bring out the agenda, one copy each and ask if there's anything on the agenda they want to bring to the front of the meeting.

An agenda will also help us get back on track if, as a result of a discussion with our client, we get sidetracked.

I mentioned in Chapter 5, the importance of using positive language and an agenda gives us the opportunity to do just that. Rather than putting subject headings such as pensions or life insurance on your agenda, use phrases that emphasise the benefits of our products and services. People in business don't usually want to retire so talking about pensions and retirement is something of a turn-off!

The agenda I use looks something like this:

Meeting between Lee Clarke and
John Client on 1st December 2008
at John Client and Company

AGENDA

1. Burning Issues

2. Family/Business News

3. How your Money is doing

4. Staying on Track

5. Review of Priorities

6. Action points

The Burning Issue

When dealing with business owners - and families for that matter - I've found over many years that there's almost always a 'Burning Issue', something that is occupying a large part of our prospect's mind, often distracting them and even keeping them awake at night. Experience has taught me that whilst such an issue exists, our prospects and clients are unlikely to take more than a cursory interest in what we have to offer.

As a result of this, and as I lay down the agenda in front of my client I will ask:

"Before we get into the main things we've agreed to talk about today, is there one Burning Issue, something in your business or in your personal life which is distracting you at the moment, possibly waking you up at 2 o'clock in the morning so you can't sleep properly?"

Mostly our clients will shake their heads and confirm, "No, there's nothing particularly concerning me at the moment". In some cases, however, they will say yes indeed there is, and then go on to explain that they are having difficulty with a particular employee, a supplier that's letting them down, some problems with the health and safety executive or difficulties with the bank manager. After a few years in the profession we should have a number of connections in various different areas of business; maybe one of these could be of assistance to our client. I have found that even if our contact is unable to help, the response from my own clients to my offer of help, and an introduction to an outside contact that's unconnected to my own business and where I'm not financially involved in the outcome, is very much appreciated and it elevates my reputation in the eyes of the prospect or client making future business dealing that much easier.

A couple of years ago, I was personally introduced to a director of a large national house-building company. At our first meeting I asked the Burning Issue question, and it transpired that my prospective client had a paraplegic son. His son needed care 24/7 which cost a great deal of money to provide. At the same time I discovered that my client had not made a Will. I realised that the death of my client or his wife, or a serious critical illness, would have devastating consequences for their son and I stressed that until they had made Wills and had put in place an Enduring Power of Attorney, my advice on other aspects of his financial planning would be superfluous.

We agreed to reconvene at my office a week later, along with my client's wife and a Trust lawyer who I introduced and who had specialist knowledge in this particular area. I offered to leave the meeting for a while to give them a chance to sort things out, but my client requested that I remain.

About an hour later, with the help of email, the lawyer's secretary and my assistant, the Wills were printed out and produced in my office for our clients to sign and for me and my assistant to witness.

The Wills done, we then continued with the rest of the agenda!

I mention this example because it illustrates how seriously we should take matters such as Will planning and that we should make every effort to ensure that our clients have their legal affairs properly in order. In the UK, most of the people I meet have little idea of the effects of dying without a Will and the complications this can cause the family.

Recently a long-standing client died unexpectedly while on holiday. He had been expecting to retire within a couple of years. Although he had given me the impression that his Will had been done it transpired that it had not, so he died intestate. Fortunately his family all agreed to a Deed of Variation and with the assistance of another lawyer the family affairs were sorted, enabling the widow to continue to live in the family home and with financial security. It may not have been so straightforward!

Going back to our agenda, item 2 - Family & Businsss News - is really just a friendly way of doing some fact finding for those all important soft facts, along with an update on any births, marriages, deaths etc. within the family, or within our client's business. These days, as more of my clients have grown-up children and grandchildren, the news comes thick and fast! David has moved to New Zealand, Fred is working in the United States, Steve is learning to fly, Grandpa finally sold his shares etc. All these bits of news are enormously helpful in transacting future business.

Item 3 on the agenda, How your Money is doing, is where we introduce a review of our client's existing investments and retirement plans. For a new client, this could be the result of our gathering all the data following an initial meeting, and where we're now able to feed back to our client the all-important information that has rarely been given previously: a consolidated report on everything the client has.

Where this is a review meeting for an existing client, this a good time to make sure that any changes that may have happened in the client's circumstances highlighted in the previous question can be taken into consideration when reviewing the appropriateness of the existing investment portfolio.

From time to time, our clients' funds will have fallen in value. We should not be afraid to discuss this and to explain to our clients the reasons for it. The majority of our clients should understand that a falling stock market is a buying opportunity. Over the years, by making sure we manage our clients' expectations in this respect, we should obtain considerable amounts of additional business at times like this.

Item 4 on the agenda, Staying on Track, gives us an opportunity to review our clients' medium- and long-term goals. After all, if this is an existing client, then we should have notes from previous meetings to enable us to discuss our client's original goals and objectives. Once again, the information given to us by our client when discussing the family and business news should enable us to help our clients decide whether these goals and objectives need reviewing.

Finally, Action Points are where we decide who is doing what. Presuming there is some new business to transact, we will have our own action points. However, if there are pieces of information or actions that our client has to do, possibly to consult with another member of his company, or put another one of his friends or contacts in touch with us, it is important that our client leaves the meeting with these items clearly recorded.

Chapter 15
Sharpening the Axe

Most people know the story of the two woodcutters, both chopping trees in the same wood, yet one woodcutter who took regular breaks ended up felling far more trees than his companion. The reason was that when he took breaks he not only refreshed himself, he also sharpened his axe. It's very important for us to allocate time to self-improvement and professional development – our own 'axe- sharpening time'. Those of us who work for insurance companies will usually only get training from our own company and that training will mostly be limited to the products and services offered by that one company. When we work in a profession such as that of financial adviser it's important for us to be fully aware of the much wider picture, covering local tax law, the products available from other companies, and the measures clients can take with their own finances that do not necessarily involve a product of any sort. We should therefore attend open conferences when available, such as those run by our professional associations or by specialist companies where not only will we gain this valuable additional knowledge but we will also make contact with people who may be able to assist on those rare occasions when we are unable to help with a particular client.

The importance of MDRT

For the last 25 years I've been a member of MDRT - *Million Dollar Round Table,* the premier association for financial services professionals worldwide. Whilst local professional and company meetings enable us to keep up with technical and product ideas, the

MDRT annual meeting enables us to understand more about what's happening in the world as a whole and, most importantly, to learn those 'people skills' which, in the UK at least, are so rarely taught at company or professional association level.

It's been said that being successful in our profession involves 90% people knowledge and 10% product knowledge, although you have to know 100% of that 10%! Our companies will usually provide us with the whole of that 10%, but rarely will they address any of the 90%. I strongly recommend that all of us involved in financial services should make it part of our business activity to qualify for and attend the annual meeting of MDRT. Doing so will raise your business to a new level of professionalism and achievement. MDRT is many things to many people. Some find inspiration and become highly motivated by the main platform sessions. Others have learned how to deal with changes in regulatory and tax laws as members from other countries share their own experiences and highlight not only the pitfalls but also the many opportunities arising from such change. Speaking for myself, some ten years ahead of the changes in the UK distribution model I was able to learn from Australian and New Zealand delegates how they managed the identical changes currently being introduced in the UK. Preparation ensures we are ready and can fully embrace changes which cause near panic and misery among others. I still find it extraordinary that many UK advisers give as the only reason for not attending, that 'It's too American', whatever that may mean.

Whilst attending *the Strategic Coach® Program* in Canada I found myself sitting next to another financial adviser from my own city whom I had never met and whose company was completely unknown to me. It transpired that my new-found acquaintance worked in a particularly rare area of financial advice and tax planning. After getting to know him a bit better, he has become an important part of my network and we now introduce clients to one another.

Chapter 16
Dealing with the Unexpected:
lateral thinking

Going back to the Burning Issue question, I remember one of the first cases of this that I came across, which was rather amusing. I was dealing with two brothers that I had come to know quite well who ran a performance car accessory business. I arrived to talk to them about their financial planning and, in this normally convivial office, you could have cut the atmosphere with a knife. It was quite clear something was wrong and so I launched straight away into the Burning Issue question. It transpired that the two brothers, who had equal shares in the company, could not agree about a photocopier; one of them wished to buy a copier, the other wanted to rent one. Apparently the stalemate had been going on for three days.

I said to them, "Tell me, if there were three of you, how would you have dealt with this issue?" They replied that the matter would have been dealt with by a simple majority. I plunged in with a suggestion: "Why not appoint me a director of your company for 15 minutes only and then you can give me the casting vote?" I said this with something of a grin on my face because I did know them very well and I knew that this was just a matter of sibling rivalry and that, underneath it all, their relationship with each other was extremely sound.

There was a stony silence for quite a few minutes, then one brother broke the ice by saying, "Would you really do that?" I replied, "Of course!" So, they duly appointed me a director of their company, minuted the appointment in the company's books and they showed me the information regarding the options available for the copier. I pointed out to them that, at that particular time, there was a tax advantage to them in leasing the copier rather than buying it and so the decision was made. I resigned immediately as director.

They put the kettle on, we had a cup of coffee and the atmosphere returned to its normal state of relaxed conviviality. I was able to proceed with the rest of the agenda and I completed the business that I had called on them to do.

Shifting priorities

On another occasion, I returned to see a couple who had become clients a year earlier. Once again, an agenda had been prepared and I was expecting to discuss some savings plans because the couple were both working, had no children, and had previously told me that they had no intention of ever starting a family.

On asking the Burning Issue question, my clients told me that their whole approach to financial planning had changed since his eleven-year-old niece had died from terminal cancer just five months after diagnosis. Unfortunately his sister was unable to have any further children, and my client and his wife felt that they really wanted to have a child, something that was diametrically opposite to the opinion they had expressed at our first meeting.

This changed the course of our financial planning advice and the emphasis shifted to life and critical illness cover, rather than on shorter term savings.

Rescuing clients from a bad decision

About 15 years ago one of my clients asked me if I could help a colleague of hers, a divorced lady who was quite keen to build up some wealth. The problem was that the lady was about to invest some money in an ostrich farm! My client was convinced this was probably a bad idea and thought that I might have a more practical idea for this lady's investments.

I met Jane at her flat and she brought out all the paperwork for the ostrich farm investment; it all seemed to stack up. One of the promoters of the scheme was a bank manager who said he had checked it all out, including the people behind it and he was satisfied it was a good scheme. The problem I had was that the ostrich farm was in Belgium and, from the investigations I had made, it didn't seem as though ostriches would breed in the Northern European climate.

Fortunately Jane accepted that this was a risky investment and she proceeded with something far more mundane, but a lot more predictable. It transpired that the ostrich farm did, in fact, fail precisely because the ostriches would not breed and all the people who had invested in the scheme lost their money. I never found out what happened to the bank manager!

Jane made some additional investments in property and we meet three to four times a year to make sure everything is on track. Incredibly, Jane is still working at the age of 73 in an executive position with an educational trust and we are now restructuring her investments to reduce the impact of inheritance tax on the eventual transfer of her assets to her children. Whilst I have no doubt that Jane will continue to enjoy life to the full for many years to come, planning ahead is key and provides our clients with peace of mind should the unexpected happen.

The important message in this story is that if I had considered the ostrich farm investment to be a good idea, I would have confirmed this to Jane even though it would not have earned me any money. My original client knew this, which is why she put Jane and me in touch with one another. It is important that we are honest with our clients even if it means that we may not be able to do business on that particular occasion.

Chapter 17
Communicating Complex Things
in a Simple Way

The bucket with a tap

With all the tax and product complications that can exist within our profession, and the documentation we are expected to go through with our clients, it can all seem extremely complex. Success in this profession can depend very much on our being able to explain complex things in a simple way. We can do this by way of a combination of stories - many of them from our own experience, or that of colleagues - and we can also do this by using simple analogies. Life insurance for example has often been likened to a lifeboat, a parachute, a safety net, an umbrella - all very good ways to describe how life cover can protect people.

In what some people call the 'good old days', all the life insurance products in the UK were guaranteed: that is to say the amount of the premium was guaranteed not to change for a set amount of life cover. In the UK it is now very hard to find such a product, the majority of our long-term life products being subject to premium reviews - either with renewable term insurance, or flexible whole of life (Universal Life). I discovered a long time ago that the easiest way to describe a flexible whole of life policy was to describe it as being like a bucket with a tap.

Premium

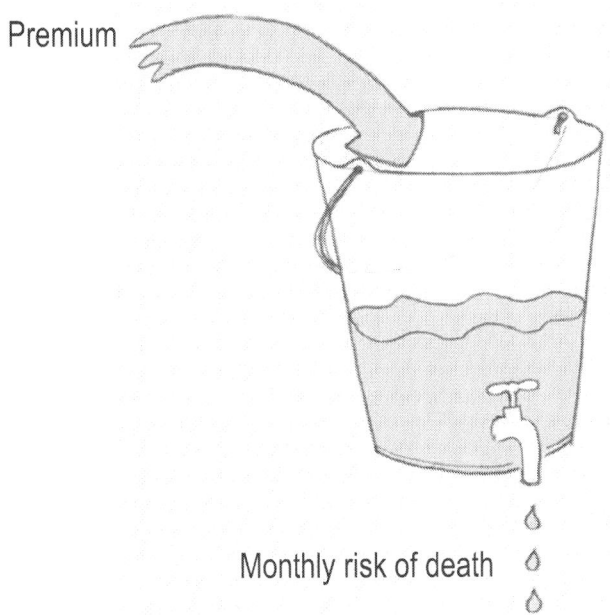

Monthly risk of death

These products are often sold incorrectly as savings plans, which they most certainly are not. However, they do build up a cash value although this is only as a consequence of how the product works. By drawing a bucket with a tap on the side, I am able to describe how the premium is placed in the bucket, where it is invested in a choice of funds. The tap is opened a little bit in the early stages when the insured is quite young, and the insurance company dribbles off just enough of the premium to cover the risk of the individual dying during that particular month. Gradually, as the policyholder gets older, the tap is turned on a little more to cover the increased risk.

I point out to people that, in the first few years, the bucket may appear to fill up as a consequence of the premiums going in, along with a positive investment return. If, however, the premiums going in are insufficient to meet the demand of the money being drawn out through the tap, or if the investment return is insufficient, then the policyholder may have to put more money in the bucket.

I find this a fairly simple concept to explain, so simple in fact that almost all my clients associate me with this particular analogy. Indeed when I was discussing my stationery with a printer client and I was looking for inspiration for a logo, he suggested it should be a bucket with a tap on the side!

Neapolitan ice cream

Quite frequently, we are asked by our clients to put together an investment programme for income.

This may be within a retirement plan or it may be a stand-alone portfolio. This then brings us into the challenging area of explaining all about asset allocation. Many of my clients have no real interest in such matters, and just expect me to recommend the appropriate investments. I do stress to them, however, that they must grasp the basics, and I've found the Neapolitan ice cream illustration to be extremely successful.

It is important if we are to use this analogy as part of our soft fact finding, that we first establish that our client does like ice cream! Draw a vertical column with four boxes in it

Strawberry
Chocolate
Mint
Vanilla

Ask your client what is their favourite flavour and write that down at the top of the page in the first box. Run through the various flavours in their order of preference. In a recent example, the favourite was strawberry, the next favourite chocolate, the next favourite mint, and finally vanilla. Write these in the appropriate boxes, the least favourite at the bottom.

Explain to your client that the vanilla is the cash and low risk securities section of their investments, the next flavour up will be bonds and fixed interest securities, the next one could be property, and the top one, their most favourite flavour, equities.

Now, many of our clients could be concerned about equities and I deliberately make this their most favourite flavour. It is important our clients learn the importance of equities in a balanced portfolio, so if they have any reservations at all, I find that by making this their most favourite ice cream flavour, this subliminally starts to relax them.

I explain that their income will generally come from the vanilla, or cash part of their investments, and the growth in each of the other sectors or flavours will cascade down into the cash pot to keep it topped up.

I explain that equities are the most volatile and yet, over time, have proven to be the most successful and effective investments for the long term and that we will not always get a profit from the equities or in this case, the strawberry ice cream. For that reason, we only transfer a profit when there is one, and this makes sure that they do not draw on that part of their investments if the fund has fallen in value. After the market chaos of 2008 this is very helpful.

Eat your greens!

Sometimes we meet people who simply say that they don't like life insurance or they don't like equities. If they have children, ask them, "Do your children always eat everything that you give them or are there some things on the plate that they don't like?" Most clients tell me that there is something, usually green vegetables, that the children don't like. Ask them what they say to their children under such circumstances. The reply is usually, "I tell them to eat their greens because they are good for them." We should explain that equities, or life cover or whatever it is that the client is not particularly fond of, are just like the greens on their child's plate and that, whether they like them or not, they are an important part of a balanced financial diet and that everybody needs some, it's just the proportions that will vary according to circumstances.

Your life illustrated as days of the week

When talking to people about planning their retirement, think in terms of breaking their life down into days of the week. Monday, they're a small child, Tuesday they're at school and college, Wednesday they get their first job, Thursday they get married and have children, Friday their children have grown up and left home, and now they'd like to have Saturday and Sunday off! Most of the people we meet are somewhere between Wednesday and Friday on this timeline and, depending on where they are, this analogy helps bring home the urgency of the situation.

Chapter 18
Personal Introductions

It is generally accepted now around the world that the very best form of business marketing is word of mouth, and the very best clients for our businesses are those to whom we are personally introduced. A personal introduction is more than a referral. Many of us have been taught to obtain referrals by asking for the names of three people we can approach who are known by our new client. We will have been given an introductory script to use when we call these people who will usually have no idea who we are, and they may or may not appreciate our call. In some countries it is difficult to make calls for referrals because, increasingly, the telecommunications and direct marketing regulations in the local jurisdiction prohibit unsolicited calls.

A personal introduction can be harder to obtain, however when someone calls you and says, "John Smith told me I should call you because he believes you can help me," it's very difficult to see how we would not do business with that person, unless somehow we create the wrong impression when we first deal with them.

So how do we obtain a personal introduction? The key is firstly to understand that we don't need as many personal introductions as we do referrals! This is because statistically we may only do business with one in three referrals but we should do business with nine out of ten personal introductions!

The second thing is that some people will naturally introduce us to others, whereas other people are not that way inclined. This is nothing against us personally, it's just human nature. We should however make sure that people understand that *we appreciate introductions* as this enables us to spend the majority of our time helping our clients. When we are talking to a client about this, we should be saying, "...and this means we can spend most of our time helping you."

In the English language, the word *appreciate* is very powerful. We should use it quite deliberately to describe the type of people we want to meet; saying "someone who would appreciate the service we offer" is much better than asking to be introduced to "someone you know who ..." It is important that we check regularly to make sure our own clients appreciate the service we give because, frankly, people will not pay for something they don't appreciate.

It is vitally important that we make it clear to our clients that we are not easy to get hold of and that we only deal with people who have been personally introduced. We do not want someone being embarrassed by telephoning and asking to talk to us only to be told that we are not available. It is, therefore, of the utmost importance that we teach our clients how to introduce people by using the 'magic words'. What magic words? Why, your name! Give them a script such as, "When you call to speak to Lee Clarke, you must mention my name because he only deals with people to whom he has been personally introduced and it is my name that will get you through the door."

Your clients will love the fact that they are placed in the position of being key to one of their friends getting an appointment with you.

One of the best books on personal introductions has been written by Dr Paddy Lund, a dentist from New Zealand who has refined the personal introduction to a fine art. Patients cannot even get into his building without a swipe card shaped like a slice of apple and he is so choosy now about the new patients he takes on that he only allows certain patients to refer people to him based on the quality of previous introductions. I'm not suggesting that we become that selective at this stage; however we should not under-estimate the power of personal introductions and the fact that, at some stage in the future, we hope to be in a position to be highly selective about who we see and which of our clients will be allowed to refer people to us!

To summarise this subject, receiving business by way of personal introductions is another step in massively increasing your own reputation as a trusted financial adviser.

Chapter 19
Professional Introductions

A number of financial advisers tell me they have had trouble making a success of professional introductions. One of the most fundamental problems that I've come across is that advisers seem to expect to get 100% of the business from any particular firm of accountants or lawyers. Frankly, this is completely unrealistic. First of all, this would actually be a phenomenal number of cases, far beyond anything we could possibly handle. Secondly, other professionals need to keep their options open, just as we do. Just as we would want to speak to a large number of accountants and lawyers, so do they want to speak to a large number of financial advisers. The reality is that, just like ourselves, they recognise the importance of people being able to get on with one another, so when I talk to an accountant or a lawyer, once I've established my professional credibility and competence, I focus on suggesting that they should bear me in mind when they come across a client who they think may get on with me. This has resulted in a quite staggering increase in introductions and, most importantly, introductions to people with whom I do indeed get on, thus increasing the prospect of business. In fact, I can honestly say that I cannot remember the last occasion when I was introduced to somebody on that basis where business did not result.

Some people have told me that you have to introduce seven people to an accountant or lawyer before you will get one introduction in return. I have not actually counted but very often I do offer the first introduction as this is quite a good way to meet another professional for the first time. Recently I was looking for a specialist divorce lawyer to assist a client of mine whose own lawyer had died in the middle of dealing with a case. I asked one of my colleagues if they knew anyone and was directed to a particular firm. I checked them out on the internet: their website gave me plenty of information about the individual partners and I telephoned the person who appeared to be most suitable. This led to that particular lawyer taking on my client and, to my delight, my name being circulated around the practice as a financial adviser who would be happy to assist any of their clients.

I disagree with some of my colleagues on the subject of sharing remuneration with an accountant or lawyer. Given the scenario outlined above you can see, I'm sure, that most other professionals would much prefer to be introduced to the occasional new client. In some parts of the world - India for example - enormous pressure is put on advisers to share commission or fees with professional introducers and even with clients. It used to be exactly the same in the UK. For some reason it seems that, especially with commission, this is seen by some as a form of extra payment (over and above what I've never been able to work out) rather than as the entire turnover of a business. When I started in the profession I was asked regularly to share my commission. I'm glad to say I never devalued myself by doing so even though, from time to time, it lost me a potential new client. However, when we start down a slippery slope it's almost impossible to stop. I want a lawyer or accountant to introduce me to his client because I'm the best person to do the job, not because I've given him a back-hander.

I'm certain our clients feel the same way. I'm indebted to my good friend Richard Usmar who gave me the perfect answer to such requests.

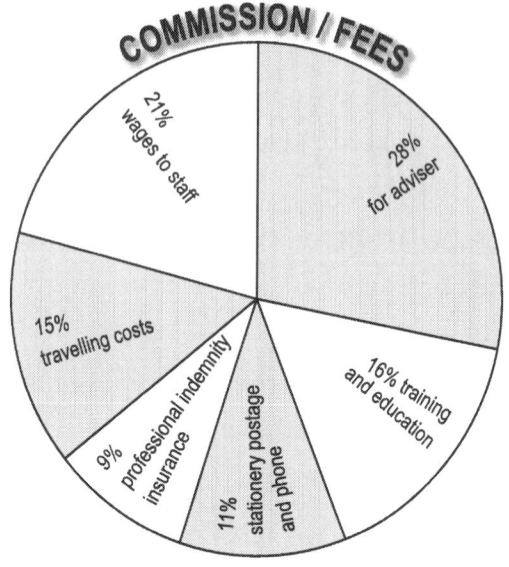

As you can see from the chart above, only a fraction of the total commission or fee is actually received by the adviser so, if pressed on the subject, I would simply show the chart and ask, "How much of my 28% do you feel you should have?" In almost every case, the request for a commission share is dropped. The proportions in your case may be different, however I recommend you construct your own pie chart so you are ready should a request be made for a share of your earnings.

Of course not every introduction we receive is perfect for us, however I never turn them away.

I received an introduction to Jonathan about seventeen years ago. He was about to go overseas to work and had a certain amount of money to invest; his lawyer, who had just prepared his Will referred him to me for advice. Although I tried to persuade Jonathan to take my advice about the investment of his money, he was particularly cautious and decided to leave the money in the bank. However, he did ask me if I could arrange an annual travel insurance policy for him which is not something I would normally do but, in the circumstances, I agreed. Although I earned nothing from it Jonathan was delighted with what I did. As it happened, Jonathan's luggage went missing on the way to Geneva and he needed to make a claim on his travel policy. The insurers were typically indifferent and quite difficult to deal with and so, once again, I offered my help and his claim was settled. I had still not earned any money from Jonathan when he asked me if I could introduce him to an accountant; I referred him to Duncan, my own accountant, who was very happy to help Jonathan. From time to time, Duncan would tell me that Jonathan had been back to the UK and had sent his regards to me. It was seventeen years later that Jonathan finally returned to the UK for good, having decided to retire. He had amassed a small fortune overseas including a significant pension fund and wanted advice. He told me he had been so delighted with the way I had assisted him all those years previously and felt it was only reasonable that I should now reap the rewards of my patience. I can tell you that I was quite taken aback and it did confirm to me the value of maintaining contact with people. The work I did for Jonathan over the next few months generated a significant five figure sum.

Maurice

Many years ago I received an introduction from an accountant in London to his uncle who was a self-employed sales agent. Although he had been fairly successful throughout his life he had never placed much emphasis on retirement planning and now, at the age of 60, Maurice was getting a bit worried about his retirement. When I went to see him I asked my usual question about the Burning Issue. Maurice confided that he felt that as long he was well enough to work he would probably continue to do so. He was realistic enough to appreciate that he would not be able to accumulate sufficient money to enable him to stop working altogether and that his main concern was that, if he died prematurely, his wife Barbara would have quite a hard time. I set up some life cover - not a lot but it was an amount that Maurice could afford - and I was able to arrange the premiums so that he could get a tax deduction on them. The accountant who introduced me was very cross with me for selling life cover to his uncle but I stood my ground and said this was precisely what was wanted. Two years later I got a call from Barbara to say that Maurice had died. He had passed away some weeks earlier and the funeral had already taken place; Barbara telephoned me to thank me very much for persuading Maurice to have the life cover as it was going to make all the difference to her. I explained to her that I did not have to persuade him, and that it was Maurice who had actually told me his main concern was to provide for her in the event of his premature death. Although this was only a term insurance policy and therefore did not acquire any form of cash value, the death benefit of £50,000 was achieved by the payment of just £800 in premiums. A pretty good investment based on the adage that *'The best investment is the one that pays the most when you need it the most'.*

Chapter 20
The Value of Networking

Networking consists of two words, NET and WORKING. I meet many people who tell me they've had no success with networking. This is usually because they don't work their net! As you'll see from this chapter, I believe successful networking depends on being prepared to make the first move, to make the first introduction.

We should never promise to bring business to our clients; however, there is nothing wrong with making sure we have a really clear understanding of exactly what it is our clients do, and the type of customers or clients they are particularly looking for. They will appreciate the fact that we take the trouble to ask and, even if we only manage to introduce them to one person, they will really appreciate this and will often reciprocate with further introductions to you. Introducing one of your other contacts to a client has an additional benefit: the introduction would normally be very much appreciated by the other party you bring into the matter.

Involving specialists

Networking can be really beneficial within our profession. A few years ago I had no facilities to deal with Group Pension Schemes and I used to refer such enquiries to a colleague. He understood that he was only to deal with the Group Scheme and to leave me to deal with the personal requirements of my clients and their colleagues. This proved to be a very good idea and worked to our mutual advantage until quite recently, when my Group Scheme colleague retired which coincided with my having the capability to take on this type of business myself.

For some time I have introduced mortgage business to another specialist rather than transact the business myself. The mortgage broker and I do not share fees, however he does refer back to me any people introduced to him by my clients and keeps me informed of the progress of all cases so we can co-ordinate properly the associated protection insurance policies.

We really do need to understand how much our clients appreciate the introduction of others to them. Having built a reputation as a trusted adviser by always being honest with our clients, they should be able to rely on us to introduce people we also believe to be honest and who do what they say. I'm not pretending that we can always come up with the right introductions from the first day we start our businesses, however this is also where networking meetings come in. Attending networking meetings such as breakfast clubs, Chamber of Commerce, BNI, Ecademy and so forth enables us to meet people who may be able to help our clients and prospects. This is where the 'two ears and one mouth' principle comes in once again. All too often I attend such meetings and find people so keen to tell everyone what they do that they are not listening at all to what others do. I find this is the main reason why people are unsuccessful at face-to-face networking.

It's also a mistake to give up too soon. People tell me they went to this or that meeting three or four times and never got any business out of it. Three or four times is simply not enough - unless, of course, we determine that the people generally attending these meetings are not our target market.

Become a regular at the meetings, so people get used to seeing you there. Be seen to be reliable. Remember what Dan Sullivan says, as mentioned earlier in this book, that to get referrals we have to be referable!

To do this he says we simply need to:

- Show up on time

- Do what we say

- Finish what we start

- Say please and thank you

This applies particularly to networking as people are unlikely to refer anyone to us unless they feel we are reliable and referable. In the early days of my business I built some of my most valuable long-term clients and connections through regular involvement with my Chamber of Commerce. As your network grows never be afraid to weed out people who prove to be unreliable. Your own reputation is at stake here and it's important to ensure that everyone working with you meets your high standards.

In conclusion with regard to networking, WORK your NET and you can be assured of a quality stream of personal introductions. As I mentioned at the start of this chapter, we only need a fraction of the number of personal introductions compared to the number of referrals, simply because someone personally introduced will probably get on with us and will probably need our services right then.

Chapter 21
Safety in Numbers

For many years I believed that being successful would be the automatic consequence of being professional and that being professional simply meant that, being so good at my job, business would automatically come my way! The fact is nothing comes our way automatically, we have to go and get it! I have this discussion regularly with some of the financial planners in my own country where any suggestion that we might have to sell something is seen as unprofessional. I mentioned in Chapter 3 that when we talk to people about what they want we are helping them to buy; however this is still a sales process. Persuading somebody to become a client is a sales process. Getting people to introduce their friends and business associates to us is a sales process. To manage our business activity properly we must *know our numbers*. By this I mean we must know how much money each client earns us in a year and how much money we earn on average through each appointment or meeting that we have. We must know how many meetings we have with a client or prospect in order to complete the business and we must know how many people we need to talk to in order for one of them to become a client.

For many years I tried to deny this simple fact until my good friend and mentor Tony Gordon eventually persuaded me to accept that by keeping track of these very important numbers not only would I be able to detect any change in the trend in my business, very quickly I would also become more effective in the use of my time.

We do not need sophisticated computer programmes to do this. A simple notebook is all that is required to keep track of our daily and weekly activity. All we need to do is draw some vertical lines on the page and list down the left-hand side the numbers of appointments we need for the week ahead, another column for the name of each client as the appointment is made, the date of the meeting and, if the meeting is cancelled or postponed, somewhere to record that fact. Finally we record the earnings (if any) from the meeting. It's very easy from this to track our business activity.

Some people prefer to fill the list of appointments from the bottom of the page upwards and thus avoid the possibility of leaving any uncompleted spaces.

I have met many successful advisers from all over the world and if there's one thing that differentiates them from people who are less successful it's the fact that they keep track of their activity.

In 2002 I started tracking my activity much more closely. For many years I had been producing business at MDRT Court of the Table level but had never quite made it to Top of the Table. On analysing my activity I discovered to my alarm that, whilst my average case size was quite large, it was taking me approximately five meetings to complete each piece of business! I realised that some of these meetings were completely unnecessary because I had simply failed to prepare properly, resulting in unnecessary additional meetings. I decided it was time to review the way I worked. I started to have a telephone appointment with my prospect in advance of the meeting so that I could get a better idea of exactly what we would be discussing at the meeting. This meant I could be better prepared with the necessary product alternatives and various illustrations to meet my client's requirements. In the UK we cannot complete any business with a client unless, at the meeting, we are able to give the client an accurate illustration of precisely what we are recommending.

It is partly for this reason that I also have as many meetings as possible in my office because if the illustration is not precise enough, or an additional product is required that I did not previously foresee, my office can prepare the paperwork during the meeting.

As a result of carefully monitoring my activity and making better preparation for meetings, I was able to reduce my average of meetings to two and the additional time saved is used in meeting further clients or in taking some well-deserved time off!

By that simple expedient I was able to increase my production to Top of the Table level, which has been maintained ever since.

Most of the successful people I have met have their own favourite systems for tracking their activity; however I find Tony Gordon's system the simplest.

Halley's Comet effect

Some years ago I was fortunate enough to witness one of the rare appearances of Halley's Comet in the night sky. The glow from the comet is caused by minute dust and ice particles as it passes through the outer atmosphere and, whilst the comet itself is highlighted as a bright ball of fire, the tail that follows it is approximately 30,000,000 miles long. Likewise in our business activity there will be occasional balls of fire represented by a really large case. The rest of what we do will be much, much smaller. Sadly I come across too many people who believe they can exist on large cases alone and, in the same way that Halley's Comet can't exist just as the ball of fire without the much smaller particles, so it is with our business. Again, looking at the truly successful people in our profession we find that they do indeed have some large cases but the bulk of their business is at a much more modest level. Once again this highlights the fact that it is activity that counts, not focusing on large cases.

There is a children's game where you take coloured blocks of different shapes and put them into holes of the same shape; managing our activity can be much the same as this. Having decided what days in the week and which weeks in the year we are not working, we have to make time for what I referred to earlier as the 'axe sharpening' activities. Our diaries should look like a crossword puzzle of blocks which have to be filled up, much like the children's game. When we know how many appointments we need in a week we simply have to fill up the blocks of activity and make sure we do not go home at the end of the week until the following week is full up.

Certainly some appointments will be lost through the occasional client not showing up or cancelling the meeting and we may have to cancel the occasional meeting ourselves.

Personally I prefer to refer to these lost appointments as postponements rather than cancellations because whenever they happen we usually simply move the appointment rather than cancel it outright.

Chapter 22
Working for our Clients

When anybody asks me for whom I work, I respond that I work for my clients. The fact is whether we are self employed, work for a life insurance company or bank or for a large national independent adviser, ultimately it is the client for whom we work. I would also say that in my experience I have never known someone become more successful by switching companies. There is an old saying 'a poor workman blames his tools' and this is just as true in our profession. When we are trying to build our reputation and gain the trust of our clients and prospects, we achieve completely the wrong result when we criticise the products that they already have or make disparaging remarks about the previous advice they have received. One of the reasons for this is that when we do so we are actually questioning our clients' own judgement, and this is hardly a good way to build a firm and solid relationship with them.

I am quite surprised when I find out that many advisers do not bother to establish the details of and reasons for the existing financial products owned by our clients. Irrespective of whether or not we were able to deal with the companies involved, it takes very little effort to establish what these policies are, what they do, and why our client took them out. We can then place these on a schedule so the client has a single sheet summary of everything, showing what they're paying, what is paid out should they die, what is paid out if they don't die, who gets the money and why the product was taken out in the first place.

When I asked why a particular policy had been arranged, the client told me that his father had been in the business and had arranged the policy early on in his career. The father had subsequently died and his policy was one of the ways in which they were constantly reminded of how much he cared for them. My goodness, how much trouble I would have been in had I dived in and criticised that policy before getting all the facts!

Chapter 23
Delivering Proceeds

Tony and Janet

I've already mentioned the importance of being there for the delivery of proceeds from protection policies such as life insurance and critical illness. One of the best and most moving examples in my own experience relates to an income protection claim. To tell this story it's necessary to go back a few years. Tony and Janet had been referred to my partner Morwenna and in their first meeting it transpired that Tony had previously suffered a brain tumour. Naturally, he assumed he would be uninsurable, however it had been some years since the tumour and the doctors had given him the all-clear. Morwenna managed to get him insured for income protection. A couple of years later Tony started showing signs of forgetfulness; this was causing him to lose his job and he called to say that they would have to cancel the insurance. Morwenna urged them to keep the policy going and suggested putting in an insurance claim. It transpired the tumour had returned. The claim was successful. The doctors gave Tony two years; he lived for four and the insurance paid out every month until his death.

Tony's funeral was a celebration of his life. Janet wrote a touching letter to Morwenna thanking her for persuading them to keep the policy going and telling her that they attributed Tony's extra two years to the complete absence of financial worry as a result of the insurance. During those two extra years Tony also enjoyed the arrival of two new grand-daughters.

Never too young for life insurance

Sometimes the benefits of our products come to light rather sooner that we expect. Sarah was only 19 when I met her and she was engaged to James, a national hunt jockey. I arranged some life insurance for both of them and, as they were not married, I placed the policies in Trust to ensure the proceeds would go where they were intended. Only a few months later, Sarah's fiancé was killed in a riding accident. Apart from the insurance that he had arranged through me, he had taken out a further policy through the Jockey Club which he intended to be for Sarah's benefit. However, as this policy had not been placed in Trust, the proceeds fell into his Estate and his parents took all the money refusing to give any of it to Sarah. Whilst this was most unfortunate, at least Sarah was able to benefit from the policy arranged by me and whilst nothing could replace the man she loved, she was financially secure. A couple of years later Sarah met another young man and they eventually got married and moved away. Unfortunately I have lost touch with them now.

Josie was only 17 when I met her and her fiancé David. They were buying a house and had planned to get married the following summer. I arranged life cover on them both and, once again, as they were not married I placed the policies in Trust. A few months later during a terrible storm, a tree fell across the road in front of David's car and he was killed in the impact. The couple had been planning to improve the house they had bought and being their first home it was in need of considerable work. Josie decided to use the proceeds of David's life insurance to complete the work on the property and landscape the garden, as well as clearing the mortgage. When the job was done she decided not to stay in the property but to sell it. She felt a sense of closure because she had been able to complete the project that the two of them had started a couple of years earlier. She commented to me later that she would never had been able to do this without the life cover and if she had not been able to complete the project she would have had a much more difficult time dealing with the loss of her fiancé.

Sarah and Josie were my first two widows; their combined age was just 36

At this point I must say I despair at the very small number of advisers in the UK selling life insurance for anything other than debt clearance or inheritance tax. Being cynical, I might guess that this is because it *does* have to be sold! I attended a meeting of advisers which had been convened by a leading insurance company to get feedback on their future product development. A number of advisers around the table could see no place for whole life insurance. I can't understand this at all, any more than I can understand financial advisers not selling this magic product. Anyone from outside the UK reading this would wonder how anyone in our profession could fail to sell life insurance; however that's what happens when relative prosperity in the nation makes it possible to offer investment products to people searching for them rather than going looking for prospects for life insurance. This is not a book about how to sell life insurance, or why from a customer's perspective you should have it. Anyone needing ideas in that direction will find plenty of books and audios on the MDRT website, or through Amazon.

One of the great joys of this profession is seeing our clients become successful and witnessing the effects of our products and services in action. When I met Owen and Katherine they were both working very hard, living in a small terraced house filled with second-hand furniture. From an early stage, however, it was clear that they valued financial independence and they sought my advice on mortgages, savings plans and retirement planning.

As time went by they started a family and, in due course, moved from their small terraced house to a very spacious individual property in a nearby village. In tandem with the increase in their standard of living they continued to increase their savings and also accelerated the repayment of their mortgage, resulting in the clearing of the mortgage in half the original term.

Their young children are blissfully unaware of how fortunate they are to have parents who will not be dependent on them in later life!

On one of my visits to the MDRT meeting in America I bought a pack of joke one million dollar bills. Sometimes I give them to the young children of my clients saying, "As long as your parents keep taking my advice then one day they will be able to give you a real one of these!"

Chapter 24
He who Makes no Mistakes
makes Nothing

This is an old adage, the origin of which is lost in time. Making mistakes is a fact of life and everybody does it. What's important however is that we admit our mistakes, learn from them and move on.

Sometimes this even means admitting a mistake which is more of a misunderstanding than a mistake; however in accepting responsibility for the mistake, we can build our credibility and enhance the trusting relationship with our client at the same time.

I can remember when I came up with a better value term insurance policy for a young couple, saving them a few pounds a week over their existing policies. They had lost touch long ago with the original adviser and I felt that I was doing them a good turn by offering them something of better value. Now, I'm not generally a superstitious person, however one thing I will not do is cancel somebody else's life policy for them. In cases such as this for example, I will advise the clients to continue to pay the premiums on the existing policy until the new one has been fully underwritten and is in force. Then the clients can cancel the original policy if they wish.

On this occasion the new policy was underwritten quickly and put in force. About two months later, my clients telephoned me to say that they were concerned to see that they were still paying the premiums on the old policy, which they thought I was going to cancel. I reminded them that it wasn't my normal practice to cancel somebody else's policy and that I felt certain that I had told them that they would have to do this themselves. The clients were quite adamant that they did not recall my making such a suggestion; however they agreed to contact their bank immediately and cancel the direct debit and I offered to refund the over-paid premiums from my own pocket. This only cost me about £30, which was a fraction of the commission I'd received on the new policy. Strictly speaking, I did not need to do this but it showed that I was prepared to accept responsibility for the misunderstanding, and this small gesture resulted in my being introduced to another member of my client's family who was considerably better off, and who became one of my best clients.

On another occasion, more recently, a new client had been introduced to me by his lawyer for an Inheritance Tax plan. My prospective clients were quite wealthy, having several millions of pounds on deposit spread around various banks. After I had presented my recommendations, they advised me that they felt it would be best for them just to 'try me out' at first with a relatively modest amount of their money, and see how things went. Anybody who knows the North of England will realise that there are some very shrewd people in that part of the world, and these people were among them! I remember with some amusement that when they were totting up how much money they had, his calculation came to around £2.7 million, until his wife said that she'd got another £1.4 million in a number of building societies. Anyway, they wrote a cheque for £200,000 and the paperwork was completed. I then went back to my office and the clients went off on a month's holiday. When I submitted the business, I discovered to my consternation that the insurance company in question would not process the cheque from the clients without seeing copies of bank statements showing the origin of the money. Now, I'm a reasonable person and I understand that, in these days when anti money-laundering regulations are so rigorously enforced, they have to be certain where the money's coming from. However, as the cheque was drawn on Lloyds Bank it seemed to me that in all probability that's where the money was. If it wasn't, the cheque would surely bounce. No, that wasn't good enough for the insurance company; they wanted to see that the money was in the bank via a bank statement. Crazy or what? There was no way for me to contact the clients, and this cheque sat in a drawer in the insurance company's office for a full month. Needless to say, on their return from holiday the clients were not happy. They had lost the interest on the money that had been on deposit prior to moving it into their current account to cover the cheque and this did not bode well for my new relationship with these people. I thought for a moment and decided I had to do the honourable thing. I told them I would send them a cheque personally for the interest they had lost on the money over that month, since it certainly was not their fault - even though I also considered it was not entirely mine!

Subsequently I was able to get most of this money back from the mutual fund company after almost a year of arguing so I wasn't completely out of pocket.

However, the gesture made by me, which would have actually cost me all the commission on the case, fast-tracked my relationship with this couple and the next time I saw them they gave me a much larger cheque to invest! Key to the importance of this was the speed with which I paid the money to them. There was no reason in my mind why they should have to wait months while I argued their case with the investment company.

Quite recently a client of mine who I mentioned earlier in this book was concerned to discover the extent of the charges that had been applied by an insurance company on a recently arranged retirement plan. I had to admit that I'd never come across a case like this where such a substantial charge had been taken at this stage in a contract. However, it was clear from the original paperwork that it had been disclosed in the small print and it was an oversight on my part that had led to this not being drawn to the attention of the client at the outset. Once again, I wrote a cheque to the client from my own funds to cover the charges, even though these had not been paid to me in the form of commission.

My client said to me that I did not have to do this; I said that I am not a normal financial adviser, that I treat my clients fairly and I like to think this is why they continue to deal with me. He agreed that was so and went on to introduce me to one of his very wealthy friends with almost £3 million to invest. Now I should stress that I don't treat every case in this way, however almost all my clients have introduced me to others and the value of this network is considerable. Sometimes it pays to lose money, or at least make a modest sacrifice in the interests of the whole business; over the years, I have found that this approach has paid me back handsomely. In fact I remember during the 1990s there was a particularly unsavoury campaign going on to flush out inappropriate advice with personal pensions. Like so many things, it all started out with the best of intentions: to look for isolated areas where people had been given inappropriate advice, but it developed into something of a witch-hunt. Every policyholder had to be written to, to ask if they felt that they had been given bad advice. If they failed to respond they received another letter, then another letter, each one placing greater emphasis on the potential compensation they could receive by agreeing to a review. In some instances people were even telephoned to ask why they had not returned the forms sent to them. One of my clients, Mark

McGregor, had a heated exchange with the caller saying that he had never questioned the advice he received from me and that he wasn't about to question it now. He fully accepted that, looking back, it was easy to see that a particular course taken may not have been the best one; however, at the time the decision was made, it was based on the facts at the time. He expressed his annoyance at the persistence of the people carrying out the review.

I have mentioned this particular case subsequently to quite a few people including clients and prospects. I have learned that mentioning this incident is a good way to get the message across to potential clients that we can only base our advice on present day circumstances and that people must ask their financial adviser for a regular review to ensure everything is on track.

As I write this book, our government regulator is focusing on a campaign to treat customers fairly. I know I'm not alone among financial advisers in wishing that sometimes the regulators would appreciate that, just as not all advisers are crooked, it's also true that not all potential clients are honest. Fairness, like honesty and integrity, is a two-way street! The compensation culture in the UK has led to companies specialising in getting 'compensation' by using template-based letters, encouraging people to have what I call 'selective memory syndrome' in order to get a payout through being dishonest. Making a dishonest claim is fraud. Enough said.

I had just one case that fell short under the pensions review. It was not a particularly big case but what was interesting about it was that the person who claimed he had been badly advised was another insurance adviser working for a specific life insurance company. He had asked me to carry out a pension transfer on his behalf on his own pension because he couldn't do it himself. He had carried out all the research, even obtained the paperwork and completed it and handed it to me as a *fait accompli*.

I did not know he had put in a complaint to the network to which I belonged at the time until it transpired that it had been settled behind my back and I was asked to cough up £4,000 as the settlement fell within the deductible of my professional indemnity insurance policy.

The individual in question came to me a little while later for some further advice; you may not be surprised to hear that I declined to deal with him again. Integrity goes both ways!

Chapter 25
Taking my Eye off the Ball

After a few years, my business was really beginning to take off and I became complacent, believing my profits would simply keep on growing. I stopped setting money aside for my income tax and started paying it out of the following year's income. As each year seemed to be better than the year before, I forgot the importance of continually prospecting for new clients. I had become a well-known figure in the local business community, rising to president of the Chamber of Commerce. I had a weekly column in the local newspaper accompanied by my photograph. When I walked down the high street in my town or went into a local restaurant people greeted me. More people seemed to know me than I knew!

I had married again, to a vivacious redhead who enjoyed the highlife. We holidayed in the Caribbean and bought an enormous house with a ridiculously large mortgage. It was all about to go very badly wrong. In 1989 the property market in the UK started going into recession and I had no alternative but to sell the house on terms that left me with negative equity. The marriage was over in under five years and I went from living in a large five bedroom house to a rented apartment. Friends were good to me. I staved off complete financial collapse by coming to my senses and paying off my debts before I started spending any more money.

However, the worst was not over. There are always a few people around who are jealous of the success of others and who relish someone else's problems. Another adviser encouraged a client to bring a complaint against me and, although the complaint was never upheld, it distracted me for many months and further damaged my own self-esteem. I decided to part company with the people I'd been working with and make a fresh start. Fortunately my business partner at that time, Dee McVey, expressed her faith in me, encouraged me and enabled me to get through the worst of this dark period. I never stopped networking and found another worthwhile group within my target market, none of whom knew me from the past.

I was also quite staggered at the support I received from several clients who heard of the complaint and wrote directly to the Chief Executive of our regulator at the time and encouraged him to appreciate the vacuous nature of the complaint.

Networking over the years with other trustworthy advisers also paid off because I was surprised and touched at the support and encouragement from other professionals in the business. For some years I had been a member of Toptrak, a study group of leading UK financial advisers who meet quarterly for professional development and to enhance the services we give to clients. Patrick King, one of the longest-standing members, offered to enrol my business as an integral part of his, which was all that was needed to kick-start things again. I will never forget this kindness and, once again, it confirmed my faith in the idea that if we conduct ourselves with integrity then even when things get bad there will always be a way forward.

Fortunately it was not long after this that I met my future wife Morwenna who taught me another valuable lesson. She taught me that it's almost impossible to give financial advice to yourself! Morwenna went through my finances with a fine-tooth comb and found I had paid a staggering amount in excess bank charges, which she then proceeded to recover for me.

Mirror, mirror on the wall, who is the wisest of them all?

Morwenna reviewed my life and critical illness cover and got me to increase the amount of cover I had on my own life. She also realised that at the age of 50 I was putting nowhere near enough money in my retirement plan. At that time I was driving a Jaguar car while she had a very worn-out looking Vauxhall

(General Motors) that had covered well over 100,000 miles. When people commented on the fact that she had such a run-down old car her response was, "Yes but you should see the size of my pension fund!" I realised it was time for me to put my own priorities in order. This meant two years of quite serious debt-reduction, clearing my credit card borrowings followed by a significant increase in the money I was putting into my retirement plans.

During this time I had also stopped attending the annual meeting of MDRT. I felt that I had a neon sign on the top of my head telling everyone what a mess my life had become. Of course, this was entirely in my own mind!

In 1997 as Morwenna had never been to MDRT despite having qualified, I decided it was time to go back to the annual meeting and take her with me so she could experience the magic of this amazing event for herself. It was as if I had never been away, despite the fact that it was actually seven years since my previous attendance. The meeting was in Atlanta Georgia and Morwenna and I both volunteered to assist with the Programme General Arrangements committee, something we have done every year since. Attending the meeting is a tremendous experience, and yet nothing compares to what you get out of it when you become one of the many volunteers assisting with the programme. Since that time we have both served on many MDRT committees, we have assisted in the running of the annual meeting and we have both spoken to thousands of people at one or more meetings.

It was rather like being born again. I re-affirmed my values; MDRT has a very strong emphasis on ethical practices and it gave me a track on which to run. I re-affirmed my commitment to integrity which has never wavered since and promised myself that I would learn from the experience of a few years earlier and make sure it didn't happen again. I had sailed extremely close to the wind and could count myself lucky that I'd not foundered on the rocks.

Chapter 26
The Global Village

I have mentioned before the enormous benefit that I and many of my professional friends have gained from membership of MDRT and, in particular, attending the annual meetings. I mentioned previously that our business is 90% people knowledge and 10% product knowledge. I have explained the way MDRT can massively expand our people knowledge, however it is also important for us to grasp the basics of what goes on in other parts of the world in financial services and MDRT also provides just such a forum for this.

This is particularly important given the large numbers of people who, for a time at least, choose to work in different countries. My good friend Mark Hanna runs his business from Walnut Creek near San Francisco in California yet he now has an office in Hyderabad, India because many of his Californian clients are Indian businesses who chose to open an office in the USA. This led to Mark being able to develop further business opportunities in India. Indeed it became a virtual necessity because of the ease with which people move from one country to another these days.

In my own case, I have American clients working in the UK for international companies, I have British clients who have been working in mainland Europe for a number of years and I have clients who have family members in Australia, New Zealand, Canada, South Africa and other parts of the world. Being able to find out some of the basics about the tax system, retirement benefit systems and the various products available in these countries has enabled me to give them some assistance and, in due course, to introduce them to fellow professional advisers in those countries whilst, at the same time, knowing that my primary contact with that client is protected.

Of course the Global Village can be something much closer to home! As time goes by you will be surprised at how many people that we've never met know something about us. To illustrate this, a few years ago I met a delightful retired surgeon who I'll call Tom, who had been introduced to me by his accountant. Tom, like many people of his generation, took complete responsibility for the family finances. He came to see me in my office and brought with him all the paperwork to do with his family affairs. In common with quite a number of people, the investments were split roughly 50/50 between Tom and his wife Petra. I made various recommendations, however I suggested it would be a good idea if Petra was present so I could explain everything. He was quite adamant that this was not necessary, that he would go back home and tell her what was going on and get her to sign the necessary paperwork.

I was (and always am) somewhat uncomfortable with such an arrangement, however I saw little alternative but to let him do this. The paperwork all came back properly completed and the business was done. Some time later I suggested a review meeting and, once again, suggested he should bring his wife with him to the meeting. He declined and came to the office on his own. Further discussion took place and, again, I suggested that it would be a good idea for me to meet his wife. Finally relenting, Tom agreed that the next meeting should take place at his home, where I could meet both him and his wife Petra and run through everything we had done.

I duly arrived at his home to be met at the door by his delightful wife who grinned like a Cheshire cat and said to me, "You must be Lee, he's not here, he's at your office!" She could see the look of surprise on my face and added immediately, "I told him the meeting was at the house and he wouldn't have it, saying he always meets you at your office!" She then told me to come in and make myself comfortable and she would telephone him and get him to come back.

About 30 minutes later, Tom arrived back at the house looking a little embarrassed. He tried to dismiss his wife, asking her to go and make a cup of tea, but I insisted she remain in the room with us and to sit down so we could have a proper conversation. I ran through the investments and the various arrangements we had put together including a Trust that had been established for their grandson and asked her if she had any questions. She didn't and she expressed her thanks to me for coming to explain everything. We then finished our tea and I left the meeting.

I was somewhat shocked a few months later to receive a call from an extremely distressed Petra, telling me that Tom had been diagnosed with pancreatic cancer and that, at best, he had some five months to live. She said that she had no idea what would happen when he died, but would I please be able to help her. Naturally I said I would and just a few weeks later, in a much shorter time than the predicted five months, her husband passed away.

Petra telephoned me with the news, barely able to control her tears, and asked me if I would handle the calls to her lawyer, the accountant and her bank manager, none of whom she had ever met as Tom had always handled everything. Naturally I agreed. I attended the funeral and a few days later I had a meeting with her lawyer and her son. It was agreed that, between us, the lawyer and I would sort out all the paperwork. This dear lady said to me that she had no idea how she would have managed had I not insisted on meeting her at the time that I did and that she would be eternally grateful to me for standing up to her husband and insisting on the meeting. Her son has now become a client and we have also added to the Trust for her grandson.

At the beginning of this particular story I mentioned that more people know us than we know. This is where the Global Village becomes evident. Quite recently I was visiting a prospective client, a doctor, some distance from where Tom and Petra lived. I had no reason to think that they would have ever had any contact with one another. I was explaining to the doctor the way I worked, and that whilst I was currently meeting him in his office I would prefer, should he instruct me to look at their financial affairs, to have a meeting at which his wife was included. I started to explain about the previous client and he stopped me mid-sentence to say that he knew exactly who I was talking about. It transpired that the deceased surgeon's brother was my new prospect's schoolteacher and that they had maintained contact with each other since he left school. Indeed, the schoolteacher had introduced my new prospect to his brother the surgeon during medical school and they had worked together for some months. Apparently when the news came through that the surgeon had died, my new prospect had asked how his widow was coping. The story came back about this 'extraordinary financial adviser' (his words) who, fortunately, had insisted on making himself known to the family before the untimely death of the surgeon and how I had handled everything so efficiently and sympathetically. My new prospect said to me, "If you are that financial adviser, where do I sign?"

Earlier I mentioned a client who had been with me since he was 18 and who now, at the age of 40, has remarried. His new wife is American and to complicate matters further the city in which she lives is right on the border between Arkansas and Texas.

Each American state has a different tax system and in Texarkana where they live the tax system depends on which side of the street you are! I've just returned from Houston in Texas where I have arranged for one of my highly-trusted MDRT member friends to look after them as they will be moving there permanently very soon.

Another of my clients has a daughter living in New Zealand where she is now bringing up her own family. The New Zealand tax system has its problems, and it can be particularly difficult if you have assets outside New Zealand. Once again I have been able to introduce an extremely trustworthy and competent New Zealand financial adviser who lives quite close by and who can look after the interests of the New Zealand branch of my client's family, whilst respecting and recognising my primary relationship with the clients overall.

Chapter 27
Adding Value

One of the biggest threats to our business is what Dan Sullivan calls commoditization, namely the ability for everything to be sold at a price and easily attained through the internet. What sets us apart as trusted advisers is our ability to add value through the customisation of our business and our processes to make it unique - something our clients will really appreciate so they no longer buy on price.

So how do we add value? Most people dealing with high net worth clients now offer various services regarding their investments; however we have many clients who are not investment clients and we also have to develop our clients until they have money.

When you consider that among the various people our clients will deal with over the years, we are one of the few that actually has a record of their date of birth, possibly their wedding anniversary, the ages and dates of birth of their children and so forth. So one of the most basic and simplest ways to add value is reminding them of important anniversaries and so forth. Many of my business owner clients are really bad at remembering this type of thing! I always send birthday cards and cards celebrating their particular religious or traditional holidays. Of course this takes an additional level of fact finding in order to make sure we have this information firmly recorded.

We all have to arrange for our clients to have medical examinations for Life Cover so why not consider arranging to collect them and take them for the examination? Not only does this ensure the client actually attends the medical, it also makes the process less stressful and therefore increases the chance of a satisfactory outcome.

We advise our clients of what they should do to increase the probability of a successful medical examination. We do this by giving them a 'Tips Sheet' advising them among other things to avoid caffeine and alcohol, strenuous exercise and high cholesterol foods 24 hours before the medical.

I mentioned earlier about how you can enhance your reputation by networking your clients together.

Somebody once asked me whether there is a danger of any resentment within our client bank if we appear to give work to one client and not to another. In the last 25 years I am not aware of any occasion where this has happened, largely because where I have more than one client offering a similar service, I will emphasise that my wish is to introduce people to someone with whom I believe they will get on well. At no time do I suggest that any one of my clients is not up to the job. Almost all my clients are successful people in their own right and any differentiation when it comes down to choosing one over the other is either going to be on the basis of who is available to do the job, and who is mostly likely to get on with the other party. By being thoughtful and connecting our clients with people who can help them we become the most important person for them to know.

One of my clients, a young lady who was going through a particularly difficult divorce, was moving many miles away from her previous home along with her two children. She was buying a property that was in need of considerable work and she has no professional contacts in the area. I located a surveyor for her who assisted with a structural survey on the property; however he needed to pay out a fee to another specialist to look at the roots of a particularly large tree that was fairly close to the property. My client had not learned to drive at the time, had two small children and a full-time job so

I drove to the surveyor in question (a round trip of some three hours) and gave him the extra money in cash to enable the job to be done. My client repaid me later and she confided in me that without that particularly generous act on my part the whole deal would have fallen through. Fortunately for my client, and also for me, she remarried and now has six children, several properties here and a further property abroad. She now has a significant amount of life and critical illness cover and, as you can imagine, she and her husband rarely make a serious financial decision without discussing it with me.

A postscript to this story: her father is retired now, however he was previously a well-respected financial adviser himself, something that was unknown to me at the time I first met her. Evidently, she passed my recommendations to him for comment. When I met him subsequently and he told me about this it transpired that it was the added value service that I had given which was the clincher!

Sending small and unexpected gifts to your clients, especially if they are going through a difficult time, can often be appreciated. A box of chocolates, a book by their favourite author, a bouquet of flowers

- all these give the same message that we care. Many advisers send birthday cards, however I do recommend that when we do this we think about our clients, not our own business.

As you may have gathered from what has been said already, I recommend we should always attend client funerals when possible. On one such occasion, I had expressed my wish to attend the funeral of Brian, a delightful and good-humoured man whose company I enjoyed very much. On hearing that I was attending the funeral his widow asked if I would be prepared to chauffeur some of the other elderly people and then take them to the wake afterwards. Obviously I agreed, one of the ladies in question being another of my clients, a divorcee in her 70s. At the wake, I saw a small group of elderly ladies talking to each other and pointing at me. Needless to say, I thought they were discussing what a fortunate person my widowed client was in having such a caring financial adviser. Good looking too, I thought smugly. My other client, who was sitting with me at the time, went over to talk to them and when she returned she shattered my illusion by saying that they all thought that she had now got a new 'fancy man'!

A financial adviser that I know offers a service to his more prosperous personal clients of doing their filing for them! Many people receive so much mail these days, much of which confuses them, that they just leave it in piles not knowing what they should do with it. He charges them a fee for this service but compared to the price they pay for it the perceived value is actually priceless. Our clients do not care how much we know until they know how much we care and by providing added value services personalised to each client, we can demonstrate a level of care way beyond anything that could possibly be provided by a faceless organisation.

Chapter 28
A Glimpse into the Future

We are in extremely exciting times. Technology is advancing at an incredible pace. Video conferencing is moving into a new era where it is becoming widely available on a peer to peer basis and all this is happening at the same time that the cost of travel - both in terms of the oil price and the impact on the environment - are all causing us to question the amount we travel. I believe that in as few as five years' time advisers will be transacting business without leaving their home or office, using video conferencing as a means to conduct review meetings and to go through documents with clients.

What impact will that have on each of us? Well the answer to that is very much in our individual hands. Our ability to adapt to change, to offer added value, to be seen as different from our competitors on a one to one basis will determine the degree to which we are able to prosper through these changing times.

When I came into the financial services business most people were tied agents and their key role was to find and retain clients. Advice was a secondary function and, where offered, it was usually in the form of added value. In fact many insurance companies explicitly prohibited their agents from giving investment advice.

Today the primary requirement is for advice. Most training is technical and tends to attract task-orientated people whose natural style lends itself to advising existing clients or clients acquired through some form of external strategic alliance. When I started in 1981, Syd Lipworth, one of the directors of our company, told us that 70% of the commission that we were paid was for finding the clients; only 30% of it was for actually giving them advice. It does concern me that these days the shift in emphasis from people skills to technical skills has led to some extremely good advisers who are nevertheless unable to find their own clients. As a result, in the UK at least we have seen firms of Independent Financial Advisers forming strategic alliances with clubs, organisations and employers to provide advice to their members in exchange for some form of payment. Personally I regard this as a backwards step and it also turns financial advice into a commodity to be bought at the lowest price. More importantly there is no client allegiance or loyalty and it is in such circumstances that the majority of unwanted and often unwarranted complaints arise.

The speed of change, both in terms of tax and financial practice and in the rate at which people move around the world, means that however we choose to offer financial advice we will need to be able to demonstrate our competence and also our integrity.

What is undeniable is that these very changes which are leading to more prosperity around the world will mean that the advice and assistance of a trusted financial adviser will become more important than ever.

Appendix

Useful reading:

What do you do after you say "Hello"?	Eric Berne
The Conative Connection – Acting on Instinct	Kathy Kolbe
The Social Styles Handbook Find your Comfort Zone and Make People feel Comfortable with You	Larry Wilson
The Platinum Rule: Discover the four basic business Personalities	Tony Alessandra and Michael J O'Connor
The Definitive Book of Body Language	Barbara and Allan Pease
The Secret	Rhonda Byrne
The Psychology of Achievement (Audio programme)	Brian Tracy
It can only get better. Tony Gordon's Route to Sales Success	Tony Gordon

Also visit:

www.mdrt.org
www.kolbe.com
www.insights.com
read Lee's blog at www.leeclarke.biz

About the author

Lee Clarke is a successful independent financial adviser and has developed his business over many years so that he now has up to three generations of clients within some families.

Throughout his career Lee has committed himself to his profession and to raising standards through an active participation in his professional associations. He is a Past President of his Chamber of Commerce, a founder member of the Institute of Financial Planning, a founder member of the Professional Speakers Association and has served on many committees and task forces of MDRT, the professional association for financial services professionals worldwide.

Lee is in demand as a speaker and has addressed audiences in the UK, India, the USA, Canada and Europe as well as being a regular local radio contributor on personal finance matters.

2886556R00091

Printed in Great Britain
by Amazon.co.uk, Ltd.,
Marston Gate.